R. C.

Transferd to — $\frac{x \pi}{250}$

Rev. J. C. Mengles —
in memory of many
happy visits

FUNDAMENTAL CHRISTIANITY

THE MACMILLAN COMPANY
NEW YORK · BOSTON · CHICAGO · DALLAS
ATLANTA · SAN FRANCISCO

MACMILLAN & CO., LIMITED
LONDON · BOMBAY · CALCUTTA
MELBOURNE

THE MACMILLAN CO. OF CANADA, LTD.
TORONTO

FUNDAMENTAL CHRISTIANITY

BY

FRANCIS L. PATTON

PRESIDENT OF PRINCETON UNIVERSITY
1888-1902

PRESIDENT OF PRINCETON THEOLOGICAL SEMINARY
1902-1913

NEW YORK
THE MACMILLAN COMPANY
1926

Printed in the United States of America by
THE FERRIS PRINTING COMPANY, NEW YORK.

TO
MY WIFE
ON THE SIXTIETH ANNIVERSARY
OF OUR MARRIAGE,
October 10, 1925.

THE JAMES SPRUNT LECTURES

In 1911 Mr. James Sprunt of Wilmington,
North Carolina, gave to The Trustees of Union
Theological Seminary in Virginia the sum of thirty
thousand dollars, since increased by his generosity
to fifty thousand dollars, for the purpose of establishing a perpetual lectureship, which would enable the institution to secure from time to time the
services of distinguished ministers and authoritative scholars, outside the regular Faculty, as special
lecturers on subjects connected with various departments of Christian thought and Christian work.
The lecturers are chosen by the Faculty of the
Seminary and a committee of the Board of Trustees, and the lectures are published after their deliv-
ery in accordance with a contract between the lec-
turer and these representatives of the institution.
The series of lectures on this foundation for the
year 1924 is presented in this volume.

W. W. MOORE, *President.*

PREFACE

This volume is the outcome of five familiar lectures delivered in 1924 on the James Sprunt Foundation in Union Theological Seminary, Richmond, Virginia. Though since expanded far beyond the limits allowed to lectures, the author prefers to keep the personal form of address; and ventures to hope that the additional matter may make the book more useful to ministers and laymen in various churches who by reason of contemporary controversy feel called upon to consider anew the meaning of Christianity. He also desires to express his obligation to his son, George S. Patton, Esq., M.C.P., former professor of Moral Philosophy in Princeton University, and late Director of Education in Bermuda, for many helpful suggestions and much valuable assistance in the preparation of the manuscript for the press.

"Carberry Hill,"
Bermuda.

CONTENTS

FUNDAMENTAL CHRISTIANITY

FUNDAMENTAL CHRISTIANITY

CHAPTER I

THE THEISTIC VIEW OF THE WORLD

IF ONE should drift out to sea of an evening in an open boat, it is quite possible that when morning came he would not know where he was. But if he turned his face toward the sunrising he would know where the East is, and that would enable him to find the other cardinal points of the compass. There are a great many people who in matters of religious inquiry are in this condition. They are drifting, and in regard to subjects that bear directly on the great problems of being, duty, and destiny are "all at sea." What they need is a fresh orientation, but they often err in seeking it. The easy way of following the fashion commends itself to a great many. Time was when men wore dress clothes on the street in the forenoon. But no one does that nowadays, and that nobody does it is a good reason why anybody should not do it; for it is seldom that a man has the courage to make himself a glaring oddity. So William James finds it easy to dismiss a certain form of theistic belief by saying that nobody believes in that sort of a God. But this is a frivolous way of dealing with a serious question.

Faith has been built and furnished, and regard it as the sole duty of Church members to do what they can by their religious activities to increase the membership of the household. They little dream that some who are most eager to fill the house, and most successful in their efforts, are at the same time undermining its foundations.

There are men in all the Churches who are satisfied with a meagre religious feeling and regard all definite statement of belief as so much surplusage. How much of historic Christianity men must keep in order to justify their right to "profess and call themselves Christians," it may not be easy to say; but when Dr. Eucken practically tells us that we may give up every distinctive doctrine of the Christian faith and be Christians still,[1] he lays a heavy burden on Christian forbearance. With people of this sort Christianity is a feeling and God an abstraction. To love and to believe that God is love is the short and easy creed which some are proposing as the basis of Christianity, forgetting that to say "God is love" is one thing, and to say "Love is God" is a very different thing.

It is easy to see, therefore, how an atheist may call himself a Christian. It may be said that it is easier to believe in Christ than to believe in God; and therefore the "atheistic Christianity" of which I have sometimes spoken is not hard to understand. It is not difficult to believe in Jesus, to admire his

---

[1] Eucken, *Can we still be Christians?*

[4]

life, accept his teaching, and to some extent follow his example. This is a matter of history and experience. Men have seen Jesus, walked with him and enjoyed his fellowship, but no man hath seen God at any time. The deists of the eighteenth century believed in God, though they often regarded him as remote from men; but they denied the Christian revelation. Men of to-day believe in the human Jesus, but are prone to have only a vague belief in God. So that with the understanding that while what I say contains a truth it is not the whole truth, I will venture boldly to contrast the sceptic of the eighteenth century with the sceptic of the nineteenth century by saying that the former believed in God but denied Christ, while the latter believes in Christ but denies God. If therefore I am to speak effectively on Fundamental Christianity I must ask your attention in this lecture to a theistic view of the world.

i

ORIGIN OF THEISM

It is pretty generally believed that all over the world and always men have had the idea of God, and whatever differences of form that idea has assumed there is a common element in them sufficient to give a certain content to religion. The universal fact of religion is a strong argument for man's need of religion, whatever be the answer to the question how men came into possession of the idea of God. This question is often asked, it is true, in order that the answer may serve to discredit the idea, and the fact that the question has been raised for this purpose makes it proper to consider it now.

Some say that the idea of God is an inference. Let us consider that for a minute, for inferences are of different kinds. There is the inference that comes by a sudden insight, as when Archimedes in his bath discovered the great principle in physics that a floating body displaces its own weight of water, and then without further formality ran down the street crying "Eureka, Eureka." Then there is the inference which is the result of long reflection and patient research, as when Darwin published his great work *The Origin of Species*. But we may be sure that the idea of God did not have to go round the world in a book before men came into possession of it. Men were not asking one another as they met, whether they had heard that Anaxagoras had discovered God. It is quite likely that Plato's *Timaeus* made no stir among the citizens of Athens and that Aristotle's "first mover" was not a subject of general conversation.

And then there is the inference that comes by the short cut of suppressed premises and in the unconscious way whereby we learn to recognize distance, the three dimensions of space and the personality of our next-door neighbour. The plain man who asks, Who made the stars? makes an application of the causal judgment though he may not know it by that name. The man whose imagination goes beyond the horizon's rim and thinks of something ever beyond, is showing that he has the idea of the Infinite, though "Infinite" and "Absolute" are not words in his vocabulary.

It is said, too, that the idea of God is an intuition, and it may be an unreasoned conviction, though we usually give the name intuition to certain *a priori* beliefs which we not only have, but cannot help believing to be true. But in the presence of so much atheism it will hardly do to say that belief in God is of this nature. If, however, it were shown that our *a priori* ideas were developed in experience like instincts in animals, so that what is *a posteriori* in the race is *a priori* in the individual, that would not affect their value; for what we cannot help believing is part of us and we cannot very well discredit ourselves.

Again, it is said that the idea of God has come to us by revelation. Granting the existence of God, it would not be strange if he should make himself known by his own self-manifestation. Descartes said that God may be the cause of our idea of God. Teaching a Scriptural doctrine and at the same time anticipating the entire doctrine of evolution as taught by the philosophy of objective idealism, he seems in this statement to have had his finger on the keyboard of truth. Naturalistic thinkers

[7]

also tell us that the idea of God came by evolution, as if that were an argument against its validity.

But a moment's thought will show us that this view is not coördinate with those to which we have already referred. For coming slowly and by imperceptible steps, the idea of God would not the less be an inference or an intuition or a mode of God's revelation because it came by evolution, when evolution is properly regarded. The doctrine of evolution may mean one of two things: either that all change of structure in plants and animals, all advance from feeling to consciousness and from consciousness to reason, is due to certain material displacements, which of course would mean materialism and need not here detain us; or it may mean only the process referred to by our Lord when he said "First the blade, then the ear and then the full corn in the ear"; in other words, that life, consciousness, reasoning, and religion have come slowly by the necessary steps of experience. And if our knowledge of God came in this way, it would not invalidate either our inferences or our intuitions regarding our belief in Him. For if the evolution of a belief is an argument against the truth of a belief, it is an argument against the truth of evolution and the evolutionists would be the first to suffer by an application of it. Men do not reject mathematical reasoning because it has come to its present proportions by slow steps of development.

The line of progress along which men came from

simple and inchoate conceptions of God to the accepted theism of the world has not yet been made clear. Spencer thought that religion began with belief in disembodied spirits: ghosts first and gods afterwards. Some say that men started with fetish worship, and others, such as Happel, regard the fetish as a sacramental symbol of the infinite, a view which would credit the savage with a power of generalization not commonly accorded to him. Whether polytheism was a corruption of an earlier worship of the bright powers of nature, that again being itself a corruption of an original monotheism, is a question to which anthropologists have given no satisfactory answer. Whether this hypothetical monotheism was henotheism, that is, the worship of one god without denying the existence of other gods, Max Müller, who invented the word "henotheism," finds it hard to say; in fact he seems to hold two inconsistent positions, as I have elsewhere tried to show;[2] for his henotheism in the *Chips from a German Workshop* meant what Schelling called "relative monotheism," while in the *Hibbert Lecture* it stood for anarchic polytheism. Whether primitive man was a relative or absolute monotheist it is hard to say, and we must leave the discussion of it to those who write the history of philosophy *a mundi incunabulis* and inquire as Brücker did into the metaphysics of Cain

[2] "The Origin of Theism," in *Presbyterian Review*, October, 1882.

and Abel and ask whether Adam's was a pure philosophy. There is nothing to show that in the history of mankind there has not been degeneracy as well as development. The facts cited by anthropologists do not settle this question any more than you can tell by seeing a man at the foot of a mountain whether he is about to go up or has just come down.

Inference, intuition, and the indwelling spirit of God, may all have been concerned, and probably were, in forming our conception of God. That among the crudest people there can be found the elements of theistic belief—whether they be remnants or beginnings—there can be no doubt; and if in the varying forms of that belief we are led to see the presence of God within the soul as a testimony that he has never left himself without a witness, those who are reverent readers of the Scripture will find confirmation of this belief in its teachings concerning the Holy Spirit. Our reasoned theism is doubtless due to all the elements that are said to enter into our conception of God, but he is not to be blamed who thinks that the strongest reason for faith in God is found in God's self-revelation in the souls of men.

At a pan-ichthyic congress, called to discuss the origin of the idea of water, I have no doubt that after listening to those who spoke or read papers advocating respectively an original revelation, inference, and intuition, great interest was awakened

by the remarks of a hitherto inconspicuous member
who said in substance: "Much of this discussion
has been irrelevant and unnecessary, for how can
we help having an idea of water? It is underneath
us, above us and all around us. In it we live and
move and have our being, and out of it we die."
In such terms Paul spoke at Mars' Hill impressively
assuring his hearers that "He is not far from any
one of us."

Speak to Him thou for He hears, and Spirit with Spirit can meet;
Closer is He than breathing, and nearer than hands and feet.

ii

ANTITHEISM

When we are engaged in controversy it is open
to us to choose whether we shall try to prove that
we are right and our opponent wrong, or vice
versa. Of course, if we are right our opponent
must be wrong, while if he is wrong we may be
right. The former method would seem at first
sight to be the wiser one, for if to our own satis-
isfaction and, let us suppose, that of our hearers,
we have sustained our contention, there would seem
to be no point in slaying the slain. Yet there are
good reasons against this method, one of them being that the particular work of refuting adversaries
as a sequel to the main contention will awaken less
interest. A good illustration of this is the relative

loss of interest in Flint's *Anti-theistic Theories* after reading his fine lectures on Theism.

But this is not the reason for the method adopted here. For entrenched in certain foregone conclusions as an audience may be, one is not so likely to influence it as he would be were they in a more impartial frame of mind. It is therefore a good plan before proceeding with his own argument for the speaker to do what he can to shake the faith of his opponent in his own prejudgments. I am therefore at this stage of our discussion inviting you to consider with me some of the leading opinions that antagonize theistic belief.

The seekers after truth may be somewhat roughly described as scientific men and philosophers. The former deal with things, the latter with thought. These two types of men represent the most prominent forms of antitheistic belief, and speaking *more medicorum* yet without thereby bringing a railing accusation against them, I may say that the scientific men have a materialistic, and the philosophers a pantheistic diathesis. Yet the two classes here referred to do not represent all antitheistic opinion, and we shall come to a more exact classification of antitheistic views if we bear in mind that all thought is comprehended in three words: Self, the World, and God; and that all antitheism consists in interpreting the universe in one of these terms, and could be represented as panegoism, pancosmism, and pantheism. I am not using all of these words in this discussion but shall represent antitheistic belief in terms that are substantially their equivalents; namely, materialism, pantheism, and pluralism.

1. MATERIALISM. The fundamental principle of materialism is that in matter and the motions of matter we have a complete theory of the universe. Another book of Genesis the materialist does not need beyond the *fiat* "Let there be matter and let matter move." In the motions of matter, molar and molecular, all existence is explained. But, as has been already implied, there are several forms of materialism.

There is what may be called ontological materialism. All being is matter, of which the atom is the ultimate unit. The atom has kept its place in thought and research from the days of Democritus to the present moment, and current investigations of its constitution may for aught we know close the long-existing breach between science and philosophy. The philosophers have always had difficulty with the atom; for if it is extended, then no matter how small it may be you can think of half of it, and so we get the doctrine of the infinite divisibility of matter. On the other hand, if it is not extended, how can a collocation of unextended atoms make an extended world? But difficult questions are now raised as to the constitution of the atom and it is not too much to say, perhaps, that the fate of material existence is in a certain sense to be decided in the physical laboratory.

Then we have what may be called epistemological materialism; for, since the days of Locke, philosophy's problem has been, What do we mean by knowledge? If all knowledge is through sensation, then some will say that all knowledge is sensation, and you will have idealists and materialists as the outcome of the debate. It will in any event be proper to say that there can be no feeling without a feeler and that there must be a psychic side to every sensation. But the inquirer's thought may terminate in the fact that a certain material stimulus has affected a material sense-organ, and both being material, materialism results. The reply to this is, 'No feeling without a feeler; separate sensations cannot get together and make a self; and the self so made would not be material, for matter cannot feel.' Thus sensationalism may end in agnosticism or, illogical as the process is, it may end in materialism, and as a matter of fact it has so ended.

With this start upon its career it is easy to see that materialism will not stop until it subdues all the kingdoms of knowledge. Accordingly we have cosmological materialism. The materialist's problem is: Given an indefinite number of simple undifferentiated atoms, how by their mere motions they can form worlds, generate the laws of motion, create the higher mathematics of the solar system, develop life, organize species, bring forth the reasoning animal man, by and by make him a "political animal," go on to form governments, construct codes of conduct, develop religious ideas, shine in poetry and philosophy, and finally blossom in "the boast of heraldry, the pomp of power, and all that beauty, all that wealth e'er gave."

To show this is a very large undertaking, but this was Herbert Spencer's task. The specialists in science, however, have but little to say of his work so far as it deals with their own respective departments, though they quite frequently speak admiringly of it in those departments with which they are not well acquainted. I think that considering the material he had to start with Spencer has done very well, and I do not believe that it is quite fair to deny a man the praise that is due him simply because we do not accept the fundamental principle of his philosophy. The difficulty with Spencer was that he had very refractory material to deal with. Do his best, it was not in his power to teach matter to think. And when he had finished his work he was not without misgivings as to its completeness.

The most obvious objection to materialism is in the testimony of our own consciousness, the sense of our own selfhood, and the difficulty of interpreting our mental acts in the terms of material brain-changes. But if materialism was to make good its claims it had to show—or try to—that man is just a machine. So La Mettrie entitled his book *L'Homme Machine;* so Cabanis said that the brain secretes thought as the liver secretes bile; so Hartley, the father of cerebral psychology, undertook to explain the relations of mind and brain with his "vibratiuncles." But it was left to later men to give encouragement to a materialistic interpretation of mind by experiments and discoveries in the localization of functions in the brain. This was done by Maudesley and Ferrier, and the work has been carried on by later investigators. But as has been abundantly shown, you cannot identify mind with a material substance simply because a certain function of the mind is associated with that substance. Because a lesion in one part of the brain produces aphasia, and one in another part of the brain results in loss of locomotion, it does not follow that mind is just brain-substance, though men have apparently found it easy to leap to this conclusion.

This illogical inference, however, has led to a curious philosophical speculation which goes by the name of psychophysical parallelism, a theory that affirms the existence of mind and matter, but denies that they can act on each other. And so we are told that matter goes its way, and mind goes its way, each being independent of the other, but with the result that body and soul "according well, make one music as before" by reason of a pre-established harmony between them.[3]   One of the strange but not unnatural consequences of this doctrine is that each of the partners to this union, though able to keep its independence of the other, has not been able to maintain its ontological equality, and so one of them is regarded as an epiphenomenon or shadow of the other; though opinions differ on the question whether mind is a shadow of the body or body is the shadow of the mind.

Continuing our study of the forms of materialism, we proceed now to consider biological materialism.   If we imagine the distance between man and the amoeba as represented by the two *termini* of a railroad, and the various attributes of mind as passengers which get on at intermediate stations on the road, we shall find it hard to say at what point these several psychic passengers got on: feeling, power of locomotion, consciousness, self-consciousness, personality, reason.   We do not have evidence of feeling in the amoeba; most of us would doubt the existence of consciousness in the worm, though Rashdall regarded the worm as a "person."   But the dog seems to think and draw inferences, though we commonly keep the use of concepts or universals as the special prerogative of man.   But at what point of this journey mind, that is to say the mind of man, got on the train, the biological ma-

---

[3] Those who are interested in this doctrine should read a brilliant refutation of it in Professor James Ward's Gifford Lecture, *Naturalism and Agnosticism*.

terialists do not know. And because they do not
know, they affirm that it is not on. We do not
know at what point in the ascent of life feeling and
consciousness came into being. Du Bois-Raymond
said long ago, *Ignoramus, ignorabimus*. But because we do not know when mind boarded the
train, we have no right to deny that she is on.
And in view of the fact that mind is on and shows
her ticket and is demanding a seat, the materialist,
it seems to me, is in a very inconsistent position
when at one and the same time he denies her presence on the train and summons the help of his
scientific police to put her off.

In other words, and this is the biologists' case,
we see in this upward movement certain modifications of structure, we see increasing psychic function with increased development of the material
organism, we see a great difference between man
and the highest of the inferior animals; and if we
are satisfied with a material organism in explaining
the psychic side of the dog, why not be satisfied
with the material organism in explaining the psychic side of man? Well, I am not satisfied that a
material organism explain's the dog's psychology,
and if I were I should not argue against what I
know in myself from what I am ignorant of in
the dog. I am sure that the dog has something corresponding to a psychic nature, and when you can
teach him conic sections I shall have still greater
confidence in his mentality. But because I have

doubts about the dog's mind I am not going to give up my own, and, surrendering to materialism, believe that Newton's *Principia* and Kant's *Critique* were simply links in a chain of material necessity that goes back without break or possibility of otherness to the remotest ages of the past.

The sixth and last type of materialism to which I shall refer is the psychological. Beginning with Locke and coming down with various modifications to the present time, we are taught in empirical psychology how ideas arise in sensation, are increased by reflection, and multiplied by association. A new period in the history of psychology was opened by John Stuart Mill who likened this combination of ideas to form new ones to certain processes in chemistry; thence we pass to the work of Lewes and his contemporaries when the relation between the two elements in the analogy referred to began to change places, until instead of mind being the reality and chemistry the metaphor, mind became the metaphor and chemistry the reality. In other words psychology gradually became a branch of physical science. This materialization of mental phenomena has reached at last the point of absurdity in the doctrine of "behaviorism" in which we have an unqualified exhibition of psychological materialism.

Consciousness is the *enfant terrible* of materialistic philosophy. If there were any way of preventing her from blurting out the truth at untimely moments or of suppressing her altogether, there might be more hope of constructing a mechanical theory of the universe; and there are men who, in spite of the contradiction implied in what they say, are ready to express regret that consciousness had ever appeared upon the scene; for otherwise there would have been nothing to interfere with a completely articulated system of material antecedents and consequents. These men do not overstate the matter when they recognize the fact that consciousness is an obstacle to materialism; but how a materialistic universe could ever have known itself to be such, these writers and individual thinkers do not say.

The behaviorists, however, have not contented themselves with the idle wish that consciousness were dead; they have undertaken the more difficult task of showing that it does not exist. We may know by experiment how this or that physical substance behaves under the blowpipe, but consciousness is very recalcitrant to the methods of the physical laboratory; for the treatment given it is an act of consciousness, and it speaks in the effort to show that it does not exist. These philosophers insist that they have tested it in their own acts of consciousness and proclaim that it is a delusion. They write books to prove to the consciousness of their readers that there is no such thing as consciousness. But in vain. They persuade themselves and their readers that what we call consciousness is after all only a series of laryngeal movements; that, for example, when you think of a certain melody—you neither sing it nor whistle it nor hum it, but just think it—your action resolves itself into a series of muscular changes in the larynx.

Now it is quite true that if one tries, without giving any audible expression to a melody, to think it, he will produce those musculatures in the larynx necessary to the production of the tune that is in his mind. But instead of confirming the behaviorist's position it contradicts it, for though I do make the musculatures I am conscious that I make them. The behaviorist psychology seems to me to be the apotheosis of contradiction, and the latest effort of materialistic thought is the most recent invitation I have received to witness a performance of the soul's tragedy and see Reason slay herself on the altar-steps of Truth. I have no wish to be rash in accusing a psychologist of materialism. He may believe in Bain's doctrine of "a double-faced unity", or he may be a Berkeleyan as to the existence of matter and a disciple of Hume as to the existence of mind, and, therefore, a sceptic as to any reality at all. If, however, he makes his arguments and conducts his experiments on the basis of what is phenomenally known as matter, he should not be surprised to find himself classed with the materialists.

But the fact is that in spite of their denial of its existence, men believe in mind, love mind, crave the reputation of having minds of exceptional calibre, write books addressed to other minds for the double purpose of convincing those minds that mind does not exist and that their own minds thereby reveal their greatness. They worship and bow down to mind, they burn incense and offer sacrifice to mind. He that is so impoverished that he hath no oblation, chooses a tree that will not rot—that is, associates his name with one of enduring reputation —and as in the allusion referred to the goldsmith covers it over with gold and casteth silver chains until the offering is decorated almost beyond recognition, so they by their elegantly written introductions, learned commentaries, and scholarly footnotes, give a new lease of life to the author whom they admire, and with a longer radius and wider orbit give themselves a larger place in public favour. This is going on all the time. It has found ample illustration in our literature all the way from Coke upon Littleton to Caird and Kemp Smith upon Kant.

There have been men, however, who though working in the interests of materialism and still regarded as materialists, have disavowed materialism. Herbert Spencer, for example, though making matter, motion, and force the postulates of his system, has distinctly said that in his belief there is at the heart of all things an Unknowable Power which is not matter; and at least one of his discerning critics has given it as his opinion that Spencer, in spite of his disclaimers, was a theist. It has been the fashion for critics to play upon the word "Unknowable," and to say there is contradiction in the statement that this something referred to is a power and yet unknowable. Of course, something is known or believed about it or it could not be called a power. But there is no contradiction in saying that the secret of the universe lies with a Power whose ways are unknowable. There is no reason to doubt that Spencer believed this; and believing this there is in it the implication of a belief, rudimentary though it be, in a Being for whom we have no other name than God. This at least was the view of John Fiske, his most admiring disciple, whose *Cosmic Philosophy* was in the same line of thought. It is more than forty years since I said to my class that Fiske was in unstable equilibrium and would go on to materialism or back to theism; and it is more than twenty years since he published his *Idea of God*, in the preface to which he says: "I am not a materialist, I am not a pantheist, I am a believer in the living God."

Some of us remember very well when Huxley's lecture on *Protoplasm* made its appearance, and how he warned his audience at the outset that if they accepted his position they were putting their feet upon the first rung of a ladder the reverse of Jacob's and leading, so they might think, to the antipodes of heaven. He gave men good reason for thinking that he was a materialist, and materialists regarded him as their champion; but he afterwards left them in the lurch, for besides writing a book upon Hume he distinctly said that he was not sure that there was any such thing as matter.

These illustrations may be taken as showing that a naturalistic view of the world need not be materialism. In fact materialists sometimes, as Dean Inge says of The Stoics,[4] "slide into pantheism"; and it is to pantheism that I shall now invite your attention.

2. PANTHEISM. This system of thought has had a long career. In pre-Socratic philosophy it was taught by Parmenides, in modern times by Spinoza. These men represent opposite poles of opinion, however. Parmenides stripped God of all predicates and posited simple Being or the One. Spinoza started with Substance and endowed it with an infinite number of attributes. In defining God he had a right to put into his theoretical construction as many attributes as he pleased, though he admits that only two are known to us, namely, thought and extension. It is easy to see the difference between the two thinkers. If you take away from anything everything that makes it something, you have nothing; so that "the one" is simpy zero. If you give God an infinity of attributes but say that only two are known to us, then to all intents and purposes God is the sum of all

---

[4] *The Philosophy of Plotinus,* I, 127.

the forms of thought and extension in the universe; and this was Spinoza's pantheism. Spinoza then was not a materialist; mind and matter made the world, and the world was God.

The question then arises, what is the relation of thought and extension to each other? There might be three possible modes of this relation. Mind and matter might act independently. You shake the tree and the apples fall; they would have fallen in the ordinary course of nature. The winds of autumn would have brought them down. But you have put your will as a middle term between the material fact and the material forces, and so have interfered with the uniformity of nature. In doing this you have performed a little miracle, and therefore you have no reason to doubt the possibility of a greater miracle by a greater mind. So Horace Bushnell argued more than half a century ago.[5] Or, mind may be a function of matter, which of course is materialism. Or yet again, mind and matter acting independently may act according to a pre-established harmony, the same determinism being characteristic of both. This was Spinoza's position and in this he seems to have anticipated the modern doctrine of psychophysical parallelism, as appears in his formula, *Ordo et connexio idearum idem est, ac ordo et connexio rerum.*[6]

Had Spinoza recognized man as the highest

---

[5] *Nature and the Supernatural.*
[6] *Eth.* II, Prop. VII.

manifestation of God, he might have reached a theism which would at least have attained the level of the doctrine of *anima mundi* which is not necessarily pantheism. But Spinoza, like many modern thinkers, had a great aversion to anthropomorphism as his famous illustration shows. God, he tells us, is no more like man than the dog-star is like the dog that barks.[7] In this he was following the example of his great prototype Xenophanes, who said that God was not like man in either body or mind and that if oxen and horses could paint they would make their gods like oxen and horses. Religion as Spinoza understood it was the intellectual love of God; a very shadowy faith when we remember that with him God simply means the great totality of which man is a part. In his ethics, however, Spinoza seems to have limited his attention to the world of thought; and in spite of his psychological determinism he constructed a very admirable system of ethics in which he commended love as the true foundation of proper relations between man and man.[8]

Spinoza's unqualified determinism, however, in any event would have marred his religious faith. For if we suppose that in a complicated mechanism, a portion of that mechanism had the power of examining it to see how it was made, it could

[7] *Eth.* I, Prop. XVII, Schol.

[8] See the works on Spinoza by Sir Frederick Pollock, James Martineau, and Robert A. Duff.

not escape the consciousness that it was part of the mechanism, that it thought only as it was antecedently determined to think, that its belief was a deterministic belief and its doubt a deterministic doubt; and that, as antecedently determined, it might disbelieve its beliefs and doubt its doubts. But for all that, if Spinoza's theology had been as consistent as his ethics, he might have reached an *anima mundi* conception of things concerning which, after the analogy of body and mind, he might have said:

> All are but parts of one stupendous whole,
> Whose body nature is, and God the soul.

It is not necessarily pantheism to regard the material world as the drapery of the Infinite Spirit by which we see him; any more than it was pantheism for the Psalmist to say of God that He clothed himself with light as with a garment.

But I am more interested in the pantheism of a later day that is more particularly associated with the post-Kantian philosophy. The story of this philosophy is familiar. It began with a theory of perception which culminated in Berkeley's subjective idealism and in Kant reached a crisis which limited knowledge to experience and furnished us with a set of categories—Kant acting as Aristotle's intermediary—good for as many trips as we choose to take within the limits of experience, but no further. Kant said that man makes his world and that the world makes him. This reciprocal relation in order to be understood required a leap of faith. Kant did not have the courage to take it, but his successors did. It was not difficult to see that to explain this reciprocal relation of man and the world it was necessary to posit a Being who as subject would have both man and the world as object. Man and the world would then be reciprocally related in the way referred to, each being dependent on God. But if this were good reasoning it would seem to follow that the idea of God in his relation to the twin object (man and the world) would call for another Being behind God. This logical *regressus in infinitum* was halted here by positing the Absolute. But it did not remove the difficulty just referred to, for we are told that God and the world are mutually dependent in the same way that man and the world are: God, it being said, would not be God without the world, and the world would not be the world without God.

Hegel started his own system with the Kantian statement that existence is only for consciousness. From that position to the doctrine of an infinite self-consciousness the transition is simple enough if you do not try to prove it by logical process. But it is easy to see that another inference might have been drawn from the statement that existence is only for consciousness, and instead of positing one infinite consciousness, it would have been just as easy to posit an infinite number of finite consciousnesses, resulting in a monadology like that of Leibnitz or later those of Herbart and Lotze. In other words, if you leave out what some would call the *deus ex machina* feature of the Berkleyan philosophy we may have on the one hand a pantheistic and on the other a pluralistic theory of the universe.

Nothing is easier of course than to say that since we have an idea of the infinite there must be an infinite Being; in fact, it is an argument, and, as I think, a good argument, for the existence of God. But Hegel's aim was not to meet the religious needs of men by justifying their faith in God; he was trying by a rigid process of logical deduction to demonstrate the existence of an infinite Being as the ground of all existence. By a regress movement of thought in the manipulation of categories, Hegel gets back to God and finds the secret of the universe in an infinite self-consciousness. You go up and come down by the same stairway; and so Hegel tries to show that the whole world-process can be easily explained, given only the necessary laws of thought.

Let me use the despised method of picture-thinking to make my meaning clear. A stained glass window consists of bits of colored glass which are kept in proper relation to each other by a metallic framework. Let us call these bits of glass "percepts"; and the lead which with its curious configurations winds in and out among them, let us call "concepts" or categories. If we had only the frame work it would be empty. If we had the bits of glass without the framework to keep them in position they would fall into confusion and there would be no picture. Kant says: Concepts without percepts are empty; percepts without concepts are blind. This is true whatever it be that we look at. We see, let us suppose, boats in the bay, cows in the meadow, men and women in the street. How is this possible? It is the result of a partnership. Nature furnishes the bits of glass; we provide the framework. That is to say, we bring with us certain categories of quantity, quality, modality, etc., and these categories set objects in relation to each other. This is a fair account of Kant's doctrine of perception.

T. H. Green in his criticism of Hume has shown that but for these categories which are part of our nature we could not say up or down or here or there, that is to say, could not have any experience; and that if we had only sensations, what we call 'things' would have no meaning: "a consistent sensationalism must be speechless." As in the window the bits of glass would be meaningless without the frame to keep them in proper relation to each other, so the world would have no meaning for us were it not for the categories which establish relations between things we see. It is clear that it is the relations between the bits of glass in the window which gives them meaning, and that if they fell into confusion they would not constitute a picture. It is also clear that the relations between the component parts of a thing make it *such* a thing, give it meaning and determine its value. This is true of every thing, whether it be a pair of scissors, a psalm-tune, or the Sistine Madonna. But can an empty frame put glass in a window? Can it establish relations between things where there are no things to be related? This is where the Hegelian logic is baffling; for categories do not exist by themselves, but are revealed only as they perform the function of establishing relations between things. Things, however, according to Hegel are themselves only relations. And so we are brought into the difficult position of having categories which reveal themselves only as they establish relations between things provided there are things to be related. But if things are only relations, the categories can serve only to relate relations to each other; the relations themselves being created by the relating categories. The result of this would seem to be that Hegel's universe consists of a set of abstractions, that is to say of ghostly categories.

If in the window the glass cannot make the frame and the frame cannot make the glass, we might think of the window as having grown; frame and glass being organic to each other and growing together, like the parts of a plant. Perhaps then the venation of a leaf would seem to be a better way of representing the world-process than the fenestral illustration I have given. It is not too much to say that Hegelianism is a system of evolution in the terms of mind. Growth is the term which would best represent the process of becoming. But the Hegelian system of evolution is no mere copy of vegetable growth. It is a concatenated system of thought or it is nothing. The postulate of the system is that thought tends to move out of its position of affirmation into negation, and then into the union of these conflicting ideas into a higher unity. We affirm Being; we negate this idea and get non-Being. But Being and non-Being meet on common ground in Becoming (nothing on its way to be something). Once get the process of Becoming started, the evolutionary process goes on without interruption. The trouble with the doctrine of evolution as held by naturalistic thinkers is that it has no logical starting-point, and is a violation of the doctrine *ex nihilo nihil fit*. Hegel in his account of Becoming shows how to begin the Creator's work of making something out of nothing. According to him, we have only to leave everything to the eternal laws of thought. Posit Being, negate it, and get non-Being, then reconcile the two by Becoming. It is not difficult. You have only to touch the button and the eternal laws of thought will do the rest. Posit Being, then negate it, and your universe is started.

The naturalistic thinkers, however, seem to be

incredulous. They persist in their empirical method of finding the facts of evolution and never ask how the process begins. Hegel's doctrine of becoming, if they only knew, is the rock of their salvation, though it is not as our Rock, our enemies themselves being judges.

This process of affirmation, negation, and reconciliation in a higher unity, is what is known as the dialectic in Hegelian logic. If, however, it is the basis of the world-process, we ought to be able to see it in the sphere of human history. But we shall look for it in vain. The Emperor will not go to Augsburg; the Pope will not receive him at Rome. But the Pope goes to Canossa and Henry can meet him there. On its face it was a compromise, but so far as the parties were concerned it was no reconciliation. Hildebrand derived all the benefit and Henry came back worse off than when he went. Judge now the Hegelian doctrine of the reconciliation of contradictions as illustrated in history and you will find that in every case—call it dialectic if you like—it is a commonplace bargain. When Tory, Bourbon, Intransigeant, Obscurantist, or Diehard, makes peace with the opposition party he is illustrating the compromising diagonal in the parallelogram of forces; he is following the line of least resistance, whether it be for the sake of public policy or to gain a private end. If the Hegelian dialectic were the eternal law of thought we might expect to see it in nature, and Hegel did his best to find it there, but without avail; for Nature seems to abhor it as much as she was once supposed to abhor a vacuum. It is impossible to fit the Hegelian triads to the facts of the physical world without trimming and changing them so much that in their new shape they can hardly be recognized. Nature moves in her own independent way without regard for the dialectic. Heedless of Hegelian grammar, but affluent in speech, she writes history in majestic words. She composes her comedies and tragedies, her epics and idylls, without the slightest regard for Hegelian syntax. She paints her picture of the sublime and beautiful, leaving to radical empiricists the ungrateful task of coming with their stencil plates to stamp their categories on its face.

Judging it in the daylight of experience Hegelianism fails. In the transcendental dark, however, it may meet and has met with better success; for there, as Hegel said of Schelling, The Absolute is the night in which all cows are black; and, we may add, there too it is harder to see through the tricks of logical legerdemain. But the stalwart Hegelian who believes that the prophet of Jena had an inspired vision of the world's creation, is not moved from his position by popular scepticism, and when men tell him that they cannot accept at his hands a universe built in this logical way, he only rattles his categories and makes reply in the familiar words "Logic is logic, that's all I say."

Let us suppose now that Hegel has been successful in demonstrating the existence of an infinite self-conscious Being, as the basis of the universe. Think what that would mean. It would mean nothing less than that a man of consummate genius had raised the scaling-ladder of his logic against the walls of heaven, and that he had pushed aside and gone behind the curtain of God's pavilion; that he had shown the successive steps in the self-consciousness of God by which the world has been generated; that the laws of thought which are part of man's intellectual nature, have determined the actions of the Almighty, and that God not only did act but could not but act according to the programme which Hegel discovered. If this is a true account of the world-process that Hegel offers, we must give him credit for having invented a dialectical strait-jacket from which God cannot set himself free. If this system of logic is not only true but also applicable to God, then no words can adequately state the magnitude of Hegel's work. But is it true? It cannot be said that Hegel has satisfied the generality of mankind. There are those who still believe in the dualism of mind and matter, and, therefore, this idealistic scheme would not appeal to them. There are subjective idealists, moreover, and this objective system of idealism has no influence with them. There are those who find flaws in the logic and deny that the steps by which the author reaches his conclusions can all be defended.[9] There are those who say that however conclusive a logic of thought-relationship may be, there is a wide gap between thought-relation and reality. When you have completed your deductive process you have only a set of categories with an inherent difficulty involved in the idea that things exist only as they are related, and that relations exist only as you have things to relate.

Again, there will be those who say that it is not certain that the categories which determine our experience in this life, apply to the operations of the infinite God. Who can say that spatial relations in the next world will be the same as spatial relations here? We can safely say, for the laws of thought require it, that if triangles exist in the next life the sum of the angles in each case must be equal to two right angles; but whether they exist or not we do not know. The Hegelian logic is an attempt to apply the logic of experience to a transcendental world. It is an argument from analogy for which theologians are so generally condemned; with this difference, however, that while the analogical argument as theologians use it is only and always in the terms of probability, the Hegelian thinker claims apodictic certainty for his anthropomorphic and analogical reasoning. Once more; there are those who believe that the Christian religion is a revelation of and from God and they feel that the Hegelian logic does not fit the facts of revelation.

9 See J. B. Baillie, *Hegel's Logic*, Chap. XII.

It requires the exercise of a great deal of faith to believe that the Hegelian logic is demonstrative. And when it comes to a choice between Hegelian faith and Christian faith I prefer to cast in my lot with those who accept the Christian faith. We cannot easily believe that the area of God's activity is determined by the Procrustean bed of Hegelian logic, and for aught we know to the contrary it is as true to-day as when the Psalmist said it, that "his way is in the sea, his path is in the great waters and his footsteps are not known."

It is not correct, however, to say that Hegelianism is a denial of the personality of God, for there are Hegelians who have no doubt of it, and the Divine personality seems to be implied in the fact that self-consciousness is the ground of all existence. I do not wonder that this philosophy is so fascinating; and I have but little sympathy with the treatment it receives at the hands of such leading thinkers as James and Schiller. If you take this system at the appraisement of its advocates, it is nothing less than the open secret of the universe. But whatever be the price you put upon it, it is a wonderful achievement of human thought, as may easily be seen by the breadth of its scope and the plausible explanation it has given of human history in all forms of experience. Rightly or wrongly, but always in a way that commands the respect of impartial thinkers, it has put its stamp indelibly upon the history of thought. If we could believe that it has accomplished all that is claimed for it, we should have to place these items to its credit: it has shown that the great categories of jurisprudence that men once thought to have come by the slow processes of judicial decision and legislative enactment were all given us *a priori* in the laws of thought; it has given us a philosophy of history and a philosophy of religion; under the single conception of self-realization, as seen in the writings of Green and Muirhead, it has unfolded the philosophy of conduct; it has set aside the old empirical conception of the State and put Bosanquet's theory in its place; it has magnified and then helped to settle the merits of the controversy between Peter and Paul through the Hegelian method of a higher unity; it has unlocked the mysteries of the Trinity and the Incarnation with the master-key of the Hegelian triad; and it has done more than that, for when Zophar the Naamathite put the question to his class, "Who by searching can find out God?" an Hegelian, amid the silence of the school, courageously held up his hand.

But by the mention of some familiar names in British philosophy I am led to make an easy transition to another phase of Hegelian thought. This fleet of philosophy I ought to say was built in Germany, and with certain minor changes in equipment has been "taken over" and placed under British registry. In each case the commander of the ship is British, the officers speak English and say "port" and "starboard" instead of "zu links" and "zu recht," but the steering gear is the same and the hull the same; the ships are freighted with the same commodities and sail the same uncharted sea of Infinite Being.

I am not always sure whether T. H. Green was a theist or a pantheist, whether he regarded God as a person or a principle, a reality or an abstraction; whether the Deity was numerically distinct from the human soul or identical with it; and whether the world as a manifestation of God, was God or only the forth-putting of God's power. But of Green's devout spirit and Christian feeling no one can well doubt who is familiar with his writings and has read the story of his life and in particular the pathetic account of his death. It was fortunate for the history of English Hegelianism that it started under the conspicuous leadership of two such men as Green and Caird. They put a spiritual interpretation upon the world in opposition to the materialism and agnosticism of their day; and whatever may have been their attitude to specific doctrines of Christianity, they illustrated the Christian spirit in their lives and by their teaching. But this attitude has subjected them to adverse criticism from opposite quarters. The advocates of dogmatic Christianity, while recognizing the lofty ethical position of these men and the high ground they took in regard to God's hand in history, very properly took exception to their interpretation of Christianity. It is true that they saw beneath the surface of the New Testament certain ethical generalizations which theologians may have failed to emphasize, but it is also true that the Christian doctrine of the Incarnation seems with them to be regarded only as a unique embodiment of the Hegelian idea of the contact of the Divine Spirit with the human; and the death of Christ only as a supreme illustration of the ethical principle of self-sacrifice. They reduced theology to the level of ethics, instead of raising ethics to the level of revealed truth. They transposed the relative places of Christ and his followers by making Calvary a mere illustration of a universal principle instead of regarding it as a supreme instance of Divine intervention and therefore as their standard of human duty. The justice of these criticisms cannot well be questioned by any who believe in the supernatural character of Christianity; but this need not prevent us from appreciating the real work these men accomplished and the fight they made for a spiritual interpretation of life. Indeed, I value this work all the more in view of the fact that some who were their pupils seem to be expressing regret that these great masters allowed themselves to be concerned with questions pertaining to Christian apologetics. That there are those who take this attitude is I think a fair inference from what Dr. Muirhead says in his contribution to the volume entitled *Contemporary British*

Philosophy. From this and other statements in contemporary literature one gathers that British Hegelianism is undergoing some modifications.

This type of thought has hitherto upheld the reputation of "proud philosophy." It has refused to stoop to the consideration of utilitarian ends. It has never been commercialized. Mathematics will serve as an actuary in the office of an insurance company, and physics receive praise for her useful inventions from men who know nothing of her epoch-making discoveries and care little that at the present moment she seems to "dwell in the secret place of the Most High"; but philosophy, happy in her esoteric faith, has hitherto held aloof from the world of fact. Now, however, she seems to be parting with her Brahminical sense of superiority, and instead of building her New Jerusalem with categorical bricks while paying no attention to the scientific scoffers who prophesied disaster and said that her walls would crumble under the foot of the first empirical fox that should tread upon them, is willing to go down to the Valley of Ono and consult with the natural enemy of a priorism.

There is, for example, Lord Haldane, an Hegelian from his youth. I admire his accurate scholarship, profound thought, and vast erudition. It delights me to watch that prehensile quality of his mind which lays hold of all knowledge that can serve his purpose. If there is a new edition of the fragments of Heraclitus he has read it; a new book on psychology from America, which is so discouragingly full of psychologies, he has appraised it. Botany and physiology are his tools. With Riemann and Einstein he discusses the problem of the four dimensional *continuum*. With Croce's new idealism and Dewey's new realism he is on intimate terms, and as a gleaner in the field of Wordsworthian poetry he has decorated his pages with a sheaf of lines which have escaped the notice of other reapers. I have been interested in and instructed by his *Pathway to Reality,* but am compelled to say that though it is lighted by the lamps of his genius and learning there are still some dark places on the road. For example, Lord Haldane is fond of saying that self is an abstraction. Is that strictly true? When a man says "myself" he means 'I,' he means a particular being that perdures, is the same to-day that he was yesterday, that thinks and remembers. If by saying that self is an abstraction Lord Haldane means that it is a general term applicable to all human beings and perhaps to other beings besides, there may be some propriety in calling it an abstraction. But if self is the synonym of 'I' it is not an abstraction. It is a word that any 'I' uses when he wishes to distinguish between his Egoity and another man's Egoity, and so far from being an abstraction there never was an abstraction that was not made by some self. How then can an abstraction make an abstraction? How can that which makes abstractions be itself an abstraction?

If, however, the human self is an abstraction, it is not strange that God is conceived of as an abstraction too. *A priori* thinkers charge the plain man with anthropomorphism. They are not free from the charge themselves. When they say that God is Thought, or Will, or Feeling, they are imputing human attributes to him. It would help matters with those who try to understand them were these writers to agree among themselves, if they must think that one of these attributes is sufficient for their purpose. But why be so parsimonious? Why, when the trinal idea is the basis of their dialectic, do they leave out this trinal element in man when they seek to define God? How is it that they can so easily construct the conception of an adequate God out of one third of a man? Of course, the reason for this is that they are seeking to discover the basal fact in human life in order to transfer it to the Absolute.

But why again, since personality is the very essence of the individual life, do they think that an abstraction is quite sufficient when describing God? They speak of God as thought, as will, as feeling. But these are abstractions. My thought does not think, my feelings do not feel, my volitions do not generate other volitions. The basal element in man's spiritual nature may be intellect, will or feeling, and men may differ as to the meaning of

"basal." If they mean simply priority of manifestation, opinion may be divided between will and
feeling; but if by basal they mean primacy rather
than priority, there can hardly be a doubt that
thought takes precedence of the other two. The
voluntarist, however, subordinates thought to will
on the principle that we think in order to act; but
when the matter is considered simply from the
standpoint of priority of manifestation we should
have no quarrel with Mr. Bradley in making senti-
ence the root idea of absolute Being, however little
we may be able to concur with the position he took
in his great book on "Appearance and Reality."

It is given to very few men to create a universe
out of a handful of categories, and in reading their
books I may err in my attempt to think their
thoughts after them. But if feeling that no one
ever felt and that never felt anything, simple un-
differentiatd feeling, afterwards generating thought
and will, represents the Absolute, that is to say
reality as distinguished from appearance, then God
has been undergoing a process of becoming, and
whether you identify him with the world process
or not makes but little difference. If we believe
in this process of development out of undifferentiated feeling, as expressing the truth about the Absolute, then worshipping God under the conception
of the Absolute we can no longer say "Thou art
the same and thy years have no end." We shall
be obliged to conceive of the Absolute as undergoing

change and still growing. And if simple undifferentiated feeling is the beginnnig of the Godhead, wherein does it differ in value from the undifferentiated matter which Spencer supposed was the cradle of the cosmos? Wherein is the world process which consists of successive heterizations of thought any better than Spencer's generation of the cosmos by a progressive movement from incoherent homogeneity to coherent heterogeneity? But if I understand Mr. Bradley, the only reality is feeling, and the development of feeling has so proceeded that all we commonly regard as Reality is only Appearance. Is it not a strange use of the law of contradiction that leads us to say that self and not-self are only appearance? As we feel now, should we not prefer the appearances and try to keep them up rather than surrender ourselves to the tyranny of a logic that turns all forms of supposed reality into contradiction? If such results are the legitimate outcome of reasoned thinking, are they not almost enough to make us lose confidence in the laws of thought? But apart from the difficulty of thinking that simple feeling represents the Absolute, does it console us to think that after a long career as Appearance, the Absolute will one day absorb all differences, reconcile all contradictions, and settle all questions of self and not-self, good and evil, right and wrong, by merging them all in the silent sea of undifferentiated feeling?

I agree with Mr. Moberly in the statement that

the doctrine of the Absolute helps us in our quest of God, though the Absolutists err in regarding him simply as the ground of all Being instead of seeking him also in response to the demands of the causal judgment. Both methods of approach are needed, and to depend upon the doctrine of the Absolute alone is almost sure to result in identifying God with totality; subjecting Him to a process of becoming; giving us a great effect without any adequate cause and making man a part of God. Excellent as Mr. Moberly's article[10] is, it reveals some of the pitfalls which threaten the footsteps of the man who treads "the high priori road." But we cannot run away from the difficulties which inhere in speculative thought, though very often more weight is given to them than they deserve.

It is a common fault of historians that in their eager desire for a "large draught of fishes" their net "gathers of every kind" and men are classed as materialists or pantheists who do not deserve either of these designations. This is particularly illustrated in Lange's *History of Materialism* and Plumptre's *History of Pantheism*. It is not pantheism to believe in the immanence of God, for we have no adequate knowledge of God's relation to the world. The doctrine of *anima mundi* is not pantheism unless the mind of man is identified with God. It is not pantheism to believe with Descartes

---

[10] W. H. Moberly, "God and the Absolute," *Foundations: a Statement of Christian Belief in Terms of Modern Thought.*

and Jonathan Edwards that providence is "continued creation," for that may mean no more than that God upholds all things by the word of his power. To believe in an intimate relation between God and the soul is in itself no more pantheistic than what has been believed by Christian mystics, or than the doctrine of *concursus* held by the Reformed theologians. Nor is it pantheism to use the language of poetry in describing God's presence in nature. The Psalmist and the Prophets did this without incurring the charge of heresy. A man cannot well be called a pantheist who makes clear his belief in the distinction between the Infinite God and the finite self. The strongest argument against pantheism is the pronoun 'I' and no man who thinks clearly on the subject of selfhood without allowing himself to be misled by logical subtleties need surrender to pantheism. But the needle of thought's compass has its variations. Men think of God now as substance and now as an hypostatized abstraction. They picture him now as an individual and now as an atmosphere. They think of him as immanent and also as transcendent. They consider him in relation to the individual soul; now as separate from it, now as indistinguishably related to it, and again as identical with it. Men differ and even the same men have different moods. Many a man lives in unstable relations to the idea of God, his foot being on the threshold of theism while he gives a backward look to pantheism. We must be patient with a man like this until "at last he beat his music out."[11]

Closely allied to the question of God's relation to the world is that of his relation to the finite spirits he has created. Mr. Pringle-Pattison deals in a very satisfactory way with the difficulties experienced by Professor Bosanquet and Mr. Bradley in connection with the latter topic. Why finite souls exist is to Mr. Bradley something 'inexplicable,' and why they should continue to exist after death is something that Bosanquet is at a loss to know. It seems then that the Absolute philosophy after finding out the Almighty unto perfection meets with the greatest hindrance to its final triumph within the precincts of the finite soul. To the questions with which man is most intimately concerned it can give no answer beyond a choice of alternatives. The Absolutist seems to waver in the choice between being merged in infinite Being and being "destroyed or cast as rubbish to the void." The bewilderment of these eminent thinkers teaches a lesson respecting the value of the Bible, and, as I confidentially believe, there are a great many adherents of the Absolute philosophy who will find comfort in what the Bible has to say on the subject concerning which it is precisely its business to speak. The fate of the finite soul is not a matter

---

[11] Dean Inge says (*Op. cit.* I, 77) he "will even risk the epigram that pantheists generally become theists if they live to be seventy."

of doubt to the believer in Christianity. He does not crave as his portion an undivided interest in the Infinite, nor does he doubt that in the future life he will keep his separate estate in his own personality.

But when all is said that can be said in mitigation of the offence of philosophy, there can be no doubt that there is a strong tendency to reduce the soul to an abstraction, to call in question the doctrine of immortality, to doubt the perduring nature of what are called "centres of consciousness" and to drown the sense of selfhood in an ocean of infinite being. Indeed, the trouble, alike with the materialist and the pantheist, is that each has lost his soul; for it matters little whether you are found dead in the bathtub of materialism or are put to death in philosophy's butt of Malmsey wine. You are equally dead in either case.

3. PLURALISM. We are told that there has been a revival of the Berkeleyan philosophy in Great Britain, owing in part to a revolt from the extreme forms of objective idealism. It is among men of this class as well as among leading empiricists in America that we find noteworthy examples of recent pluralism. Most of us know something about the Berkeleyan philosophy. Some think that it means a denial of the existence of the external world. Were we brought to this belief we might well feel that we are walking in a vain show, that we are living in a phantom world and that we are

plans and specifications of any potential three-dimensioned world and has shown that it must conform to the requirements of geometry. What we wish to know is whether in this wide universe there was no being who understood the doctrine of gravitation before Sir Isaac Newton discovered it. Is it possible to believe that this system of mathematical relations and equations embodied in what we call the phenomenal world was through millions of years unknown to any being until Kepler and Newton discovered it? We cannot think so; and so we believe in an Infinite Being who knows the world from the beginning and grasps the whole world-process in a single synthesis of intuition. In other words, the order which exists in the phenomenal world is an argument for the existence of the Being who is the presupposition of the Berkeleyan philosophy. But this philosophy will lend its sanction to another view of the universe and that we must now consider.

The fundamental idea of both objective and subjective idealism is that except for minds there is no existence. The starting point in both systems is the individual self. But the pluralist, unlike the absolutist, does not use his selfhood to lift himself up to God and then, when it has served its purpose, treat it with ingratitude by asking why the Absolute ever so far differentiated itself as to produce separate selves, and wondering whether these separate selves are really worth keeping. The pluralist is mindful of the country whence he came, is loyal to his selfhood and stands by it to the end. Whatever, then, may be his construction of the universe, this fact of consciousness, this sense of selfhood, is where he starts. There are those who interpret the world in terms of totality and are therefore pantheists. There are also those who interpret the world in the sense of individual selfhood and, the universe being conceived of as a collection of finite spirits, are therefore pluralists. With this conception of the world in our mind it is obvious that there may be and probably are spirits above and below the human level. We may go down the scale of human life and imagine that there is a psychic side to the amoeba. We may be panpsychic enough to invest the vegetable world with soul-life, so that talking flowers and sighing trees may not be altogether a matter of poetic feeling or childish fancy; and in the free use of imagination we may have a certain feeling of tolerance for Fechner's worship of the earth-spirit of which William James speaks with such respect. We may believe that in the ascending scale of "thrones and principalities and powers" there may be angels and archangels up to God. There is nothing in pluralism to put limits to the scale of spiritual beings which constitute the universe.

If now in these various orders of spirits there is a realization of order in the world, the question will arise, How it came? Do these spirits simply recognize the order as we do? Then they ought to believe in it, as we do, and say that this is a rational world; and the tendency of such pluralism would be towards theism. Do they, on the other hand, believe that they made the order? This belief is possible. This order of the world may have come about by coöperation; and as some men are recognizing that the common elements of civilization are the result of interaction among human units and therefore say that the growing harmony in the world is altogether due to human agency, so it may be believed that interaction among the finite spirits which constitute the universe may have produced the cosmos. The logical outcome of this kind of pluralism would be atheism. Or yet again, just as we may account for certain necessary and universal beliefs among men by supposing that they have all drunk of the same spiritual rock, so we may conceive that the world's order among the finite spirits which constitute the world is due to an infinite and impersonal Reason; and the outcome of this would be a pantheistic interpretation of the cosmos.

Still considering the universe as a community of finite spirits we may believe that one of these spirits so far excels all others in power, wisdom, and goodness as to be the supreme being among the spirits. Perhaps this would represent Professor Howison's position. But this supreme being would only be a *primus inter pares*. He might be the President of the Universe, but he could not be its King.

And further still, we may consider this interaction among finite spirits as still going on, with
a tendency to reduce discords, settle enmities, produce universal harmony, and finally end in what
is called a pluralistic Absolute. This I think is not
very far from being Royce's view. As the outcome
of this we might find ourselves in a democratic universe of finite spirits, self-governing, and as we
used to say of certain hotels, managed on the American plan. This pluralistic view of the universe is
now mainly confined to a few philosophers, but
should it ever be fortunate enough to have a poet
worthy of his task perhaps he will some day sum-
mon Christmas bells to "ring in the [God] that is
to be." William James as a radical empiricist was
a pluralist and believed in a finite God. Mr. Mc-
Taggart, an idealist, makes frank avowal of an
atheistic pluralism. According to his view spirits
are both eternal and immortal. They exist in their
own right and pass through an indefinite number
of incarnations. As an empirical proof of the doctrine of metempsychosis he tells us of an acquaintance whose exquisite taste in discerning the quality
of certain wines could be best accounted for on the
supposition that he had acquired it in a previous
incarnation.[12] This I fear will be no more convincing than the poetic statement that

[12] I feel sure that I have seen this in his writings but am unable to verify it.

> Our birth is but a sleep and a forgetting:
> The soul that rises with us, our life's star,
> Hath had elsewhere its setting,
> And cometh from afar;

which Wordsworth himself described as "far too shadowy a notion to be commended to faith." [13]

This prevalence of pluralism is enough to show that Locke was wrong in supposing that the existence of a thinking being is sufficient evidence of the existence of God. On the principle that matter cannot produce mind, it was right to suppose that if a thinking being now exists there has been a thinking being from all eternity. But according to Mr. McTaggart there has from all eternity been an indefinite number of thinking beings who, self-existent, and like Melchizedek, are without father, without mother, without descent, having neither beginning of days nor end of life.

Those who are interested in pluralism should read Dr. Ward's second course of Gifford Lectures. [14] With rare knowledge of science and philosophy, with scrupulous fairness and unanswerable logic, he presents the various forms of pluralism, and though less positive than one could wish in regard to the value of theistic proofs he closes his volume with a calm, reverent, and earnest plea for theism as a rational belief, and his message to a doubting world

[13] George McLean Harper, *William Wordsworth*, II, 120.
[14] James Ward, *The Realm of Ends, or Pluralism and Theism.*

may be summed up in the Savior's words: "Have faith in God."

Pluralism may exist, as we have seen, in a pantheistic, theistic or atheistic form, but its general tendency is antitheistic; and this perhaps is because though starting properly enough with the indubitable fact of individual selfhood, it has failed to take proper account of the idea of the Infinite or Absolute which is an important factor in any attempt to explain the universe.

The mistake of both the pantheist and the pluralist is that they have put asunder what God hath joined together. They are like ships which sail from opposite ports each seeking but neither finding the one that the other left; so that the pantheist has saved his God but lost his soul, while the pluralist has saved his soul but lost his God.

iii

MEANING OF THEISM

Dr. Wildon Carr in one of his recent books[15] calls attention to the present *rapprochement* between science and philosophy. It is one of the hopeful signs of the times that these two departments of intellectual inquiry once united but long separated are beginning to establish fraternal relations with each other. Philosophy cannot ignore the work of science, and scientific men are beginning to realize

---

[15] *The Scientific Approach to Philosophy.*

man and the world being alike dependent on God, the hypothesis under consideration is not irrational, and it is, or may be, thoroughly theistic. The effect of such a view would be to make every change in the material world a manifestation of God, and this view might contribute to the reconciliation of science and religion; for there would be no sphere of scientific thought without a religious side to it and no place where we should not see the print of God's footsteps. And as Browning says that every man has "two soul-sides, one to face the world with, and one to show a woman when he loves her," so the world would have two sides, a physical and a spiritual, a phenomenal and a noumenal. Looking then at this world of colors and shapes, of articulated coexistences and successions, it is phenomenally speaking a world of mechanism; but noumenally speaking it is a world of purpose. From one point of view it is all matter, but from another all mind.

Were this a true view of the cosmos we should be really living in two worlds and we should have to keep account of our transactions with it by "double-entry"—if I may borrow a figure from Professor Flint. I give Professor Pringle-Pattison's view the hospitality it deserves, feeling at the same time that these conflicts of opinion clearly show that neither in science nor philosophy have men yet solved the problem of the universe. These debates between absolutists and empiricists serve only to strengthen my belief in the plain man's philosophy and to make me wish for a "return to dualism"—our "familiar faith" in mind and matter —as recommended forty years ago by one who wrote under the pseudonym of Scotus Novanticus. Interesting as are the tendencies in contemporary thought in respect to the relations of science and philosophy, there is nothing in them that should affect our attitude toward the theistic problem. Let us then ask, What is God? To this question several answers have been given.

Some say that God is only another name for the Absolute. If the Absolute means totality, we get back to Spinoza's view, man himself being a part of God. Some, as Lotze, make the universe to consist of God and the finite spirits which he has created. This is a perfectly tenable hypothesis, and the allegation that by creation God limits himself and becomes a finite God is an uncalled for refinement. Rashdall needlessly exposed himself to criticism in so far as he affirmed belief in a finite God for this reason. But the doctrine of a finite God is taught by Mill and Mr. H. G. Wells on the ground that evil is incompatible with the omnipotence of a benevolent God. Mr. McTaggart says, and very properly, that a finite God will not do. Obviously not; for if he is finite, why not another finite God? Why not indeed three finite Gods: a God of power without love, a God of love without wisdom, a God of wisdom without power? So we might con-

standing." If feeling is the dominant attribute in God, then we shall say with the Apostle John that God is love, that is to say, is a loving Being. If will is the word that best represents our idea of God, then we mean that God "upholds all things by the word of his power." But there is no reason whatever for thinking of God under one of our own attributes to the exclusion of the other two, though it may be now one and now another of the human attributes that we emphasize when we think of God. If, therefore, as the result of physical inquiry it should come to pass that the electron is the ultimate unit of the physical universe, and that the electron resolves itself into energy, we need not say that God is energy, but that energy is a word that denotes his manifestation, and we shall learn to see God in the home-made lightning of the laboratory as plainly as the children of Israel saw him in the lightnings of Sinai.

Toward the close of his Gifford Lectures, Mr. Pringle-Pattison tells us that "the traditional idea of God must be transformed." One wonders what result will be reached by such transformation, but the suggestion seems to put new meaning into the prayer contained in the "second paraphrase" so familiar to Scottish ears:

> God of our fathers, be the God
> Of their succeeding race.

I cannot wait for this 'transformation' but must do the best I can to answer the question, What is

God? Clearly we are shut up to one of three methods of procedure: we may exclude all attributes, include all attributes, or exclude some and include others. If we adopt the first method we reach the zero of Parmenides. The second plan would land us in an Eastern pantheism. The third is therefore the only one that can be approved, and adopting that I need no better definition than the one which is contained in the Westminster Assembly's *Shorter Catechism*: "God is a spirit, infinite, eternal, and unchangeable in his being, wisdom, power, holiness, justice, goodness and truth."

iv

ARGUMENTS FOR THEISM

Much should be said respecting the arguments for the existence of God that it is impossible to say here. But I must refer to those who complain that the theistic argument is analogical and anthropomorphic. Of course it is. How could it be otherwise? We argue in accordance with the constitution of our nature. If we had no idea of cause, no sense of the Infinite, no feeling of dependence, no idea of the world's order, no consciousness of purpose, we should be shut up to atheism. Why, then, should we be blamed for using these ideas in seeking after God?

Nor is it a valid objection to the conclusions reached in the use of these ideas to say that they are not demonstrative. They are not. We cannot transcend probability. And if we could demonstrate the existence of God, there would be no need of faith. If it were as clear that God exists as that the three angles of a triangle are together equal to two right angles, why should men be urged to believe? Let us then be satisfied with the fact that there is a preponderance of reasons amounting to moral certainty in favour of the Divine existence. What these reasons are I shall presently state. It is to be regretted, however, that so many seem disposed to close all doors of access to God except the one of which they wish to make use themselves. How many ways there are of entering into the Presence-chamber of the King I do not know, but I am confident that they are all approached by one of three roads which lead, respectively, through the realm of things, the realm of values, and the realm of ideals.

1. THE REALM OF THINGS. Argument under this head is embraced in three conceptions—Contingency, Order, and Purpose.

We may regard the world as a whole or as an aggregate of parts. Conceiving of it as the latter, it is a series of coexistences in space and successions in time. However conceived, it is the subject of constant change, and change implies a cause. If, as John Stuart Mill says, every cause is an effect and every effect a cause, it is clear that a first cause is impossible. If you explain cause by the persist-ence of Force, then the obvious consequence is that the cause of the world to-day is found in the entire history of the world before to-day; and similarly, that if we knew the exact condition of the world to-day we might, if we were very clever, predict what its condition will be to-morrow. This is the naturalistic view of causation and leads us to no theistic conclusion.

Suppose, however, that you make cause a category of the will; then the cause of the world and its changes may be an infinite number of finite wills, or one infinite will. It is hard to conceive of an infinite number of self-existent finite wills, whatever Mr. McTaggart may say to the contrary. But the order of the world is an additional reason for believing in God; for, given that order, the question is how to explain it. That the order exists is proved in the fact that the world corresponds to the most exacting form of mathematical computation. In other words, we live in a rational world. To this argument there is no alternative except chance. But there is no such word as 'chance' in the vocabulary of science, for atoms as well as worlds are held in the iron grip of uniformity: "All chance, direction which thou canst not see."

But conceding the possibility of what is called "a fortuitous concourse of atoms," too much has doubtless been made of the distinction between improbability before the event and improbability after it, as Venn shows in his *Logic of Chance*. If, for example, in an audience of one thousand persons I wondered whether *A* will occupy seat 125, I should be surprised to find him so seated; but if without raising that question beforehand, I found him seated in 125, it would occasion no astonishment. This is easy to understand. If I contemplate the probability that *A* will occupy this particular seat, the chances are one in a thousand that he will do so; and this is so whether the probability be viewed *before* or *after* the event. In other words, the element of *time* does not enter into the probability, though it may for various reasons affect our mental impression. If I put the twenty-four letters of the alphabet into a hat and they are drawn in the meaningless order *a, k, o, v, x,* etc., we are not surprised. Since they must come in some order, why not in this? If, however, I first contemplated the chances of their being drawn in this order and they were so drawn, I should be surprised, because a mathematical calculation would show it to be unlikely that they would be so drawn.

Suppose, however, that the letters of the alphabet in sufficient quantity are put into a container and that drawing them a random they spell out a page or two of Milton's *Paradise Lost,* we should be still more surprised. Conceding the possibility that the above result might ultimately be produced if the process were continued long enough, the

chances against it are so enormous that the imagination boggles at it—not simply because of the
number of possible combinations of letters, but because the result has *meaning,* and it is impossible to
believe that this meaning could have been produced
by chance. Similarly the world has a meaning that
can be expressed in intricate mathematical equations, and it would be folly to impute that meaning to chance—or, as Venn puts it, "all the paper
which the world has hitherto produced would be
insufficient for writing down the odds against the
chance production of such a world as we actually
experience." The order of the world is therefore
a strong argument in support of the idea that mind
or thought—that is to say, God—is the only rational explanation of the world. For, as Baden-
Powell put it, "What requires thought and reason to understand must be itself thought and reason."

It is not every man who needs this argument.
If, with the Hegelian, we believe that the Absolute
is "the fountain light of all our day," or with the
Berkeleyan that God is the "master light of all our
seeing," the argument from order is superfluous.
If eclipses were as unexpected as earthquakes, if
the sun rose and set in the most casual way, and
the universe were "a mighty maze and all without
a plan," the Hegelian doctrine of the Absolute and
the Berkeleyan formula *esse est percipi* would not be
affected, though it might be doubtful whether a

theistic or a pantheistic construction of the world would be more correct. But all men are not idealists, and the plain man has his rights. He is therefore justified in the belief that the order of the world is convincing proof of the existence of God.

There is still another way of looking at the world of things, and that is, under the category of purpose. To indulge in the cheap rhetorical ridicule of Lange and say that Nature blunders, that she explodes a million guns to shoot a hare, and destroys a town in order to build a house; or to say with others that because having eyes a man can see, he has no right to say that eyes were intended to see with; that because the adjustments of organ to organism and organism to environment look as if they were intended to serve a purpose, we cannot prove that they were so intended, does not overthrow the teleological argument; for the fact remains that the conditions referred to look as if they were intended to serve a purpose, and we have to accept the choice of explaining these "as ifs" in the terms of purpose or of chance. They are so many, they meet us so constantly, and in so many forms, that the theist is quite safe, despite all that is said to the contrary and conceding all that can be said for naturalistic evolution, in assigning to these "as ifs" a purposive meaning. Moreover, the force of this impulse so to regard them has a strong support in the fact that scientific men cannot very well do without a metaphorical imputation of purpose to nature, even when they refuse to regard that purpose as real and therefore as a witness to the truth of theism. That this teleological idea is embedded in the constitution of our nature is well illustrated in Kant's *Critique of the Judgment,* wherein he shows that if not a "constitutive" it is a "regulative" principle of reason; and that it is not readily dismissed from consideration, recent philosophy abundantly shows. "The doctrine of final causes," says Bergson, "will never be definitely refuted. If one form of it be put aside, it will take another." But it appears only in a very modified form in his *Creative Evolution,* notwithstanding the fine illustration of it in the "paralyzing instinct" of the Ammophila to which he refers.

We are told that this argument from final causes is a "carpenter theory" of the universe and that according to it God is conceived of after the image of a man working *ab extra.* But this is an error. If we wish to see examples of *ab extra* work we shall find abundance of them everywhere in the money-making advertisements which disfigure nature, stare at us, and invite attention to cosmetics, cereals, safety razors, motor cars, proprietary medicines, articles of clothing on amputated segments of the human form, and the old familiar faces of men and women who have found in personal ailments an easy pathway to private fortunes. In these cases we see the agent working *ab extra* at so much a day. But it is otherwise with Nature when she robes herself in the bridal dress of springtime, and meets the advancing frosts by throwing around her shoulders the warm drapery of autumnal tints. She works from within and makes no display of her materials. By what right do we subject God to crude spatial relations? And what do we know of the insideness or outsideness of the Divine Being in relation to the works of his hand?

But suppose, with Kant, we say that this argument at most would only result in giving us a finite God. What then? Must every argument prove everything that we believe about God? A Being who can weigh the mountains in scales and the hills in the balance, who taketh up the isles as a very little thing, in whose eyes the inhabitants of the earth are as grasshoppers, for whom Lebanon is not sufficient to burn, nor the beasts thereof sufficient for a burnt offering, is a Being great enough to warrant our reverence, our fear, and our love, great enough to be our refuge and strength and a very present help in time of trouble. If the design argument will take us thus far on the road in our quest of him whom we seek after, we may safely trust the completion of the journey to other helps.

2. THE REALM OF VALUES. We speak of the True, the Beautiful, and the Good, not as belonging to the world of things that can be weighed and measured and counted, nor yet as a mere phase of individual feeling, but as having an objective reality in the world of thought. Whatever the

real meaning of values may be, they are a very important factor in human life. Take them out of experience, and life would hardly be worth living. These ideas, then, may therefore be called values *par excellence*. Some find their worth in the pleasure they afford, and it is quite true that they often fall to this low hedonic level. But pleasure in their possession does not exhaust their meaning, for we have in our minds a standard of values undefined, it is true, but pointing to an objective ideal; and the question is not whether we like this picture or not, but whether or not we ought to like it. The idea of worthiness to be liked is a tribute to the inherent objective excellence of the picture or the "piece" which is under consideration. Men and women love music, but they outgrow their early ideals. It is a long way from song to symphony, and the lesson of appreciation is not easily learned. So, too, the path of achievement has been a long one, and it is the unattained that stimulates the effort of the great master.

The same is true in literary art. Men grow tired of the gaudy and the commonplace, and learn to seek refreshment of spirit from the best writers. The level of production is rising too. The great ones are always easily counted, but of the good in various degrees of excellence there is a growing number. Compare the writers of the better class with those of the ordinary type and note what gives their work distinction: taste more sedate, style more demure, verse more refined, prose more restrained; *exit* the exclamation point, vanish interjections. Note too the shy allusion seen only by the more discerning reader, the quiet humour honoured with a smile but evoking no mirth, the epigram fresh minted and shining like a new shilling in a handful of older coin, argument packed in the silver casket of a comely sentence, and words selected for their fitness but placed where they can best serve the ends of melody and rhythm. These artists in sound and speech are part of the long procession which for ages has been walking in the toilsome way of progress with their faces toward the Infinite.

Let us now turn to the moral values, which we shall consider under the idea of the Good. Suppose that all men were liars, that free rein by common consent were given to lust and that human life were cheaper even than in some places it seems now to be; should we regard such a world as a place in which one would choose to live? But without a sense of right and a feeling of moral obligation to do the right, could we expect to have even such a world of moral order as we now have, poor as it is? What, then, do these ideas mean, and whence have they been derived? Akin to this question is the inquiry what it is that we should seek after as our chief Good?

No man can wish himself unhappy, but it is a shallow answer to the question I have raised to say that happiness is the chief end of man, though it is very commonly given. Epicurus gave it and it has been repeated from that day to this. Two centuries ago Lord Shaftesbury called attention to the fact that benevolence is a factor in our nature as well as self-love, and should have a place in ethical theory; but it was left to psychologists of the last generation to show that in every child there is an egostic and an altruistic self, and to offer peda-gogic help in the training of the young. Came then the psychological hedonist to tell us that whether he will or not man always acts for his own happiness—the voluptuary and the ascetic alike—that be he squanderer or miser, it is happiness he seeks, that he foregoes happiness for the sake of hap-piness, and that in his unhappiness he is happy.

It was a long time before the idea of moral obli-gation, as distinguished from the idea of happiness or the sense of justice, assumed its proper place of prominence in ethical discussion. It came into con-spicuous use in Kant's "categorical imperative," and was independently emphasised by his English con-temporary, Price, who was the first, if I mistake not, to use the word "oughtness" to symbolize the supreme category of morality. But "oughtness" has not been allowed to speak with the magisterial authority which belongs to it, for men have tried to reduce it to lower terms; the "ought" growing up out of the "must," as some say, or standing only, according to Bain, as signifying "a strong ideal avoidance." But "ought," as I believe, is no word to be trifled with or made to serve the purpose of an empirical philosophy, and the attempt to hatch oughtness out of utilitarian eggs has been a conspicuous failure.

Then came those who said that the chief end of man is not the happiness of the individual but the greatest happiness of the greatest number. This doctrine with its differences marked the school whose leading teachers were Bentham, Mill, and Sidgwick, the last named being the one whose genius illuminated the closing period of Utilitarian philosophy. That was the time when altruism was a word to conjure with and men like Mallock gained distinction by praise of its merits and ridicule of its excesses. Philosophers from Epicurus to Spencer, like street musicians, have been playing this hedonistic tune at the doorstep of every century, each century unfamiliar with it and therefore thinking it was new. But like other more familiar and more popular melodies, we seldom hear it now; and when we do, only on an organ of obsolete design. For science has put a new song in our mouth. "Be happy," said the hedonists; but "Be strong" is the motto of the ethical evolutionists. The new ethic teaches that the sense of right and wrong is the outcome of the happy chance that enabled the race possessing it to vanquish and overcome all its enemies. That is right, therefore, which has "survival value."

I do not say that the fundamental principles of evolution are devoid of evidence in their support, so far as the physical structure of animals is concerned. But when the doctrine of natural selection is carried into the philosophy of conduct by such writers as Westermarck and Leslie Stephen, it is simply an unverified and unverifiable hypothesis based upon an unauthorized inference from the supposed demonstration of the Darwinian doctrine of the origin of species. Conceding, however, the truth of this doctrine, it is singular that by the accidents of chance it has been easier for natural selection to develop a "categorical imperative" in the human race than a scrupulous regard for it. Blind conformity to a law that is not known seems more in keeping with natural selection than a formulated rubric which is not regarded. Observation seems to show that men are more ready to recognize the value of the law of moral obligation than to practise the virtues it inculcates. Let it be granted, however, that the categorical imperative is here and the life-saving virtues also here, and, moreover, that the only reason for heeding the one and practising the other is that disobedience and non-performance would sooner or later terminate the race's career. The only reason for conformity being the desire for the perpetuity of the race, it follows that one who does not care for that, need not conform. A wonderful deterrent from wrongdoing this would be, to the man whose impulses lead him to gratify his passions! Tell him that if he and men like him continue in their evil ways the race will sooner or later die; much he will care!

But this is not all. Nature is in a fair way of being thwarted in her aims by those who minister at her altar. Through long ages, and largely by the influence of Christianity, men have been interested in the Good and the obligation to seek the Good. But now a body of men bent on disclosing the secrets of nature, are divulging that which should never have been told. For men might have been good had they simply been left to the force of the law which tells them to be good; but now that you tell them the reason for the law, you exempt them from all obligation to obey it unless they happen to have an imperious desire for the perpetuity of mankind. Look at the matter and you will see, when you have thought it through, that the existence of the moral law and the obligation to obey it resolve themselves into either a desire to be happy, a prudent expediency, an impulse to seek conformity to some vague impersonal principle of right, a regard for "survival value"; or else these virtues point to a Holy Being in whose nature they are realized and by whose law they are commanded. Truth lies, I believe, in this last alternative.

But the mention of truth reminds me that my task is not yet done, for as a supplement to the ethics of evolution we have been presented with a new conception of truth. It is obvious that truth is something different from fact. The river and the windmill that we pass in an evening's drive are facts, not truths. So are the plaster casts in one museum and the stuffed birds in another. But truth is the correspondence between thought and reality. When men say that the moral ideas of virtue and obligation are the result of a process of evolution and that they have value because they tend to promote the life of the race, they mean that their thoughts correspond to the facts. The issue between those who accept and those who deny this view of the origin of moral ideas is one in which both parties accept the same theory of truth, to wit, the correspondence of thought to reality. But we are to deal now with an entirely different conception of truth. And when men accept the pragmatist's theory, they overthrow the basis on which the evolution theory of morality rests; for truth according to the pragmatist is not the correspondence of thought to reality, but the correspondence of thought to a demand for satisfaction.[18]

The pragmatist may give respectability to his idea by likening it to the process of induction wherein the hypothesis is framed and tentatively held, pending scientific proof, until confidence in

[18] Cf. William James, *Pragmatism;* F. C. S. Schiller, *Studies in Humanism;* and for acute and entertaining criticism, Bertrand Russell's *Philosophical Essays.*

it is established by its correspondence to established fact. But his position is very different from this. The psychology of the old conception of truth was that we are dissatisfied until thought corresponds to fact. But in the pragmatic doctrine the emphasis is not on the correspondence of thought to fact, but of thought to satisfaction. We may hold any theory as true so long as it satisfies us, and when it no longer satisfies us it is no longer true. Hence truth changes. What was once true (not simply *held to be true*) is true no longer. What once worked, works no more. Hence the search for truth is search for satisfaction. It is a very accommodating theory. To the religious man it says, 'So you are satisfied you have all you can ask.'

This is the greatest peace platform for contentious thinkers that was ever constructed. On it are assembled the world's seekers after truth, and they are all told that the essence of truth is that every man be fully persuaded in his own mind. It would be worthy of Mr. Bernard Shaw's dramatic genius to place upon the stage the Agnostic, Catholic, Calvinist, Christian Scientist, Quaker and Seventh Day Adventist; the Pantheist, Pluralist, Pragmatist and Personal Idealist; the Brahmin, Buddhist, Parsee and Confucianist, in a new pragmatic play of "As you like it."

Be satisfied: that is the new gospel of peace. Be satisfied: that is the anodyne that lays disquietude to rest. Be satisfied: that is the pragmatist's message to a striving world. Ask no questions, fight no battles, have no fears; otiose and indolent, simply rest content. The inevitable logic of pragmatism is a state of intellectual quietism for some and of scornful indifference for others. Are you ready for this? If not, let us ask again, What does this world of values mean? I refuse to accept the naturalistic account of human progress, refuse to believe that seekers after truth—shut up to the necessity of looking back upon the pit whence they were digged—must see in lofty thought and high ideals only the wasteful prodigality of nature; and in the great virtues of love and justice only nature's cunning contrivance for saving our race from death. I believe that these virtues have a forward look, are an intimation within us of a great reality above us, and that as stated in Professor Sorley's happy phrase, "God is the home of values."

But men may say, 'We are not materialists, we believe in God. The only question is whether he is the *terminus a quo* or the *terminus ad quem*. We admit that the flowers of spring are more beautiful than the soil on which they grow; that art, science, and philosophy represent a higher level of being than is indicated in the experience of primitive peoples. We realize, too, how useless all this is if it all ends in death. We see that in the long result "survival value" is a matter of small moment; for the individuals of each successive generation die, and by and by, on an ice-girt earth where it will be hard to stand before its cold, the race itself will die, or perish in one of nature's cataclysms, when the elements shall melt with fervent heat. We agree with you that the spontaneous tribute men pay to science, the homage they give to virtue, and their divine discontent with attainment and achievement are prophecies of better things to come. It is a sorry picture our world presents, of hopes unfulfilled and ideals unrealized, of conflicts of opinion and contests of war, resulting in "confused noise" on the one hand, and, on the other, in "garments rolled in blood." But nevertheless, if we take love and justice out of the world it will become a wilderness of thorns and briars. Therefore, as best we can, we must conserve these values, and in order to conserve them we must invoke religion's aid and to make it attractive must enlist the service of the Beautiful.

But religion will not serve as means to end. It must have the supreme place or it will not stay. And more than that, the loveliness of religion does not come from Art, but best shines sometimes in homes where Art has never entered. These men are right, however, when they say that in order to keep the world of values they must keep religion, which really means that these values find their ultimate explanation in God. We cannot, therefore, well dispense with the idea of God whether we regard him as the cause at the beginning or the effect at the end of a great process of Becoming.

Human distinctions may come down to us or we may climb up to them, and such honours are gratifying to their recipients whatever be the way in which they come. The peer whose coronet is of recent creation and who boasts no Norman blood, probably enjoys his elevated position quite as much as the English nobleman whose name is on Battle Abbey, though one honour came by heredity and the other is the reward of industry and service. I can understand, therefore, the satisfaction that some may feel in the thought that, since the march of progress cannot be stopped, humanity is on the road to God. But I refuse to take the attitude of the pantheist who by the logic of his principles must regard himself as a part of God, or of the pluralist who thinks that he is climbing up to the same position; and rather than take either view for the sake of avoiding the materialistic consequences of the doctrine of "natural selection," I would turn the evolutionist's favourite metaphor into reality, and reading 'purpose' into that which he calls 'mechanism' regard the whole evolutionary process as evidence of God's guiding hand.

Accepting, then, the moral virtues as unescapable facts of our nature, we seem shut up to believe that the sense of moral obligation and the virtues of justice and benevolence are only Nature's tricks to save the race, or we must believe that these virtues are prophecies in us of an indefinite progress of mankind to higher levels, or else that they are imperfect reflections in us of ideals which are realized in God. In reality, however, they offer us but two alternatives. They lead us to the cross-roads of thought, and as we interpret them in a naturalistic or a spiritualistic sense, are signboards on one of which we read "This way to agnosticism," and on the other "This way to God."

3. THE REALM OF IDEALS. Nature is a scheme of finitudes. We have a rising scale of organic life, a system of values reaching to ever higher levels with no assignable limit of achievement or attainment. Nature's superlatives are such only as to the past, but are in the comparative degree as to the future. The highest is only the highest as yet. You cannot reach infinity by adding a finite quantity to a finite reality. And yet the mind will rest only in the infinite. Strain our imagination to the utmost as we may in our search for this infinite, we shall never reach it by a process of development. Let human nature advance to some unknown attainment in the future life, we cannot conceive of it as having reached the limit. One spirit may so far exceed the rest as to be the highest, and if that being be called God he can only be the first among his fellows, and, therefore, only a finite God. Or a community of finite spirits composed of the totality of finite spirits might be so harmonious as to be called the Abso-

lute, but it would only be a sum in addition after all, and would lack the quality of infinity. So that our idea of God cannot be satisfied by any advance of finite existence.

Nor are matters made better if we regard God as eternal Being which has passed through various stages of becoming. You may posit eternal matter—matter in a state of extreme tenuity—as passing from incoherent homogeneity into coherent heterogeneity; or eternal mind passing by successive heterizations from inchoate thought or random will or undifferentiated feeling into the world of variety open to human experience. In either case you have a totality of effects without any adequate cause, and the world process is throughout a violation of the principle *ex nihilo nihil fit*. If God changes from less to more, our measurements are necessarily relative, and the doctrine of relativity may extend to the universe of things, and values, and ideals. Our scale of values would point not to an infinite Being in whom they centre, but to a changing God. But what our nature calls for is a Being who is the same yesterday, to-day and forever. It is this thought which lies at the foundation of the ontological argument.

Anselm is the conspicuous advocate of this argument. Before him, Augustine had argued for the existence of God on the basis of the True, and Boethius on that of the Perfect Being. Anselm had also written his *Monologium* advocating the idea of God on the basis of the Highest Good. The presupposition of this treatise was the mediaeval doctrine of realism, according to which goodness was regarded as that quality in men which partakes of the highest goodness, as though there were some ideal archetype of goodness which finds various degrees of realization in human experience.

Anselm was not satisfied with this treatise. Perhaps there came to him the thought that the highest actual realization of goodness was not the highest possible realisation of it. The language of the second treatise, the *Proslogium*, suggests this. For he says: "I have in my mind the idea of a Being than whom a greater cannot be conceived, *quo nihil majus cogitari possit.*" Volumes have been written in criticism of this treatise, and it is a singular thing that though such fallacies as four terms, circle, and *petitio principii* have been attributed to this author, his critics have not been able to agree as to the particular paralogism of which he was guilty. To suppose, that in order to reply to Anselm, it was only necessary for Gaunilo to cite his imagined island, or for Kant to remind us that we cannot pay objective debts with subjective dollars, was to give Anselm credit for very little sense. His idea was no chimerical thought as, for example, of a winged horse. It was a necessity of thought, and not only so, it was the thought of a necessary Being. Now it is obvious that the necessity of an idea and the idea of a necessity are two very different conceptions, but Anselm combined them in a single phrase; for, he says, "this Being of whom I think, cannot be thought not to be." These words reveal the ingenuity and the value of his argument, and probably account for the misunderstanding regarding it. He had a metaphysical certitude of God's existence, and was trying to give it logical certitude; and what he meant was that we are under a necessity of thought to believe in the existence of a necessary being. The idea of the infinite was involved in it, for of this we cannot dispossess ourselves. But the idea of causality was also involved in it. It meant that we cannot be satisfied with an infinite regress of finite causes, and, therefore, that if anything exists, something must have existed from all eternity, and have in it the potentiality of all dependent existence; and further, that this Being must be self-existent.

It is difficult to escape the force of this argument. Kant admits that we are under the necessity of believing in a being that is *ens realissimum*, and, therefore, the cause of all other existence. But he says that this is only "a regulative principle of reason." If, then, it is "a regulative principle of reason," why not trust it? Kant made a distinction between "constitutive" and "regulative" judgments. The basis of the distinction was his conviction that our knowledge is limited to experience, in other words, to objects of sense; and a "constitutive judgment" is one that is applicable only to an object of sense-perception. But we cannot see God or hear Him, and his being or not being is not determined by any of the judgments which apply to objects of sense. That is plain enough. But if the regulative judgments about existence beyond sense are as much part of our nature as our constitutive judgments, how can Kant question our right to say that a necessary belief in a necessary being is adequate reason for believing in the existence of that being? I believe that Anselm was right and that Kant might have spared himself the trouble of making a futile display of metaphysical insight in the distinction between an analytical and a synthetic judgment, and the inquiry whether existence is a predicate. He might also have withheld his commercial illustration which was as irrelevant as it was obvious.

By the three roads already referred to, along which men have walked since the days of the pre-Socratic philosophy, we may still advance to the knowledge of God. Bypaths of various kinds come into them, and especially into that which runs through the realm of ideals. Ontological arguments for the existence of God have been made since Anselm's day by Descartes, Hegel, and Samuel Clarke, and (notably in our own time) by the late Professor Ferrier, who says, with a degree of confidence which is perhaps excessive: "Philosophy has accomplished her final work. She has reached by strict demonstration the central law of all reason (the necessity, namely, of thinking an infinite and eternal Ego in synthesis with all things) ; and that law she lays down as the basis of all religion."[19]

Whether we reason up or down, start with the individual consciousness as the given, or with the Absolute as the presupposition of Reason, we cannot divest ourselves of the idea of God. Anselm started with the latter idea, regarding God as a necessary Being having all perfections in himself and being the Ideal which reason craves. In this respect he differs from philosophers of a later date whose Absolute seems to be so meagrely equipped with the qualities necessary to an infinite being that we are compelled to think of it as undergoing a process of Becoming; to be then in doubt whether to regard the world as God and be shut up to pantheism, or to regard man as the highest form of God's existence and so be driven to a belief in a finite God.

In all this I may be wrong, and my mistake may be that I have not made myself sufficiently at home in the Hegelian logic. I confess to a sense of limitation in this regard, but when I am told that before I reach God I must climb up a tall ladder of categories—some of the rungs being not very secure—I confess that my courage fails me, and I can only say: "Such knowledge is too wonderful for

---

[19] J. F. Ferrier, *Institutes of Metaphysics*, 525.

me, it is high; I cannot attain unto it." And so I stay with Anselm.

V

CONCLUSION

It is to be regretted that contemporary thought has so generally abandoned the old theistic proofs, and that the impression has gone abroad that Kant has destroyed natural theology. There is no good reason for this attitude. None, surely, from science; for if the system of connectedness in phenomena be expressed as mechanism, this would not make it impossible that purpose lay behind and governed the interaction of what are known as natural causes. It could be said, however, that having explained the material world by natural causes the continued belief in teleology would be superfluous. Not necessarily so, by any means, for nothing can destroy the conviction that nature is an organic whole the parts of which express purpose in their relations to each other and to the whole.

The most that Kant said was that the categories of the understanding being applicable only to objects of sense-perception could not be used to prove the existence of a Being who transcends sense. This is obviously true. There still remain, however, the categories of the regulative reason which make it impossible for us to escape from the idea of God and are therefore a strong argument for God's existence. By no process of reasoning can we prove the existence of God as we would establish the existence of a fact in the material world or solve a mathematical problem. This is really all that Kant's criticism came to, and the truth of the statement is too manifest to need comment. This, however, does not make our belief in God an irrational faith, and it is a distinct disservice to religion when men who find that argument is not demonstrative take refuge in unreasoned belief and feel that by so much as faith lacks rational support by that much their faith is the more meritorious.

It is very common also for men who discard the physico-theological proof, to find especial satisfaction in Kant's moral argument. There is good reason for attaching a high degree of value to this argument—that is to say, the argument based on moral values—for it really shuts us up to the alternative of believing that moral obligation has no basis of authority in our nature or that we must find it in God. But if the same rigid test were applied to the argument based on the "practical reason" that is applied to the principle of the "regulative reason," the moral argument would deserve no better fate, for demonstration is as impossible under the one as the other.

But, as the late Professor Flint shows in his *Agnosticism,* the mistake of Kant was in assuming that we have two or three kinds of reason instead of the one reason applied to different kinds of objects. Finding, however, that theistic proof falls short of demonstration—and that is all Kant's criticisms amount to—some will discover in this a special reason for emphasizing our dependence on the Bible. 'Kant,' they will say, 'has proved that reason does not support our faith in God, and therefore our only hope is in Revelation.' This would not help the cause of truth, however. Those who take this attitude should remember that belief in the Bible presupposes belief in God as the author of the Bible, and moreover that the Bible proclaims the lesson of natural theology by telling us that "the heavens declare the glory of God and the firmament sheweth his handiwork."

Yet here again let me not be misunderstood, for the same facts which are of most vital interest in the Bible prove that God exists, in proving that Jesus was "God manifest in the flesh." The believer in Christianity is of all men the last who should be affected by the Kantian criticisms or should disparage natural theology. He is no materialist, shut up to the necessity of regarding himself as a mere assemblage of material atoms; and believing in his own spiritual nature he may believe that however widely the operation of material antecedents and consequents may extend, they do not destroy the force of the purposive idea from which he has no desire to escape and from which he could not escape if he wished. Nor should the Christian hesitate to reinforce his faith in God by the testimony of Scripture to the divine existence. Men write sometimes as though the book of nature is so distinct from the Bible that the first must be finished before the other is begun. Not so, however; they should be read together as mutually supporting and explaining each other.

It is good to return from the foreign shores of philosophy and get back again to the homeland of the Bible. All the more after such wanderings do we enjoy it. It is a delight once more to use its familiar speech, to sit beside its refreshing streams and feel the tonic influence of its mountain air. The better, too, as the result of our travels shall we appreciate its philosophy, not less profound because couched in a language we can understand, not less satisfying because it makes no effort to explain what the human mind is unable to comprehend. Have you learned in philosophy the doctrine of the Divine immanence? Paul taught it long ago: "For of him and through him and to him are all things." Has it occurred to us that although we may use the analogy of our own nature in our thought of God we cannot solve the mystery of his being by means of it? The Bible has told us this: "My thoughts are not as your thoughts." Has it sometimes seemed to be an act of presumption on the part of men to suppose that the ways of the Almighty must go in the grooves of their logic? Isaiah seems to have had the same opinion, for he says, "Who hath directed the spirit of the Lord or being his counsellor has taught him? With whom took he counsel, and who instructed him and taught him in the path of judgment and taught him wisdom and shewed him in the way of understanding?"

But better still, the Bible has opened the door of hope, it has brought life and immortality to light, it has strengthened the hand for toil, and soothed the soul in trouble. It has linked our nature with God's in the Incarnation. Well does Browning express this:

He who did most, shall bear most; the strongest shall stand the
    most weak.
'Tis the weakness in strength that I cry for! my flesh, that I seek
In the Godhead! I seek and I find it. O Saul, it shall be
A Face like my face that receives thee: a Man like to me,
Thou shalt love and be loved by, for ever! a Hand like this hand
Shall throw open the gates of new life to thee!
    See the Christ stand!

Do you know Him? or must you say:

Behold, we know not anything;
    I can but trust that good will fall
    At last—far off—at last, to all,
And every winter change to spring.

Winter indeed! "Now is the winter of our discontent made glorious summer by this Son of [God]." Do you know him? You may know all the 'isms' of philosophy, all the 'ologies' of science, all the 'ites' and 'oses' of pathology, all the 'ectomies' and 'otomies' of surgery; you may know the bench-made law of England and the bar-made law of Rome; you may have the statute of frauds, the statute of uses, and the statute of mortmain at your fingers' ends, together with the great progeny of judicial decisions which have descended from them; but if you know not Him whom to know is life eternal, you are poor and miserable and blind and naked. "Blessed be the God and Father of our Lord Jesus Christ, who according to his abundant mercy hath begotten us again unto a lively hope by the resurrection of Jesus Christ from the dead, to an inheritance incorruptible and undefiled and that fadeth not away, reserved in heaven for you, who are kept by the power of God through faith unto salvation, ready to be revealed in the last time. Wherein ye greatly rejoice, though now for a season, if need be, ye are in heaviness through manifold temptations: that the trial of your faith, being much more precious than of gold that perisheth, though it be tried with fire, might be found unto praise and honour and glory at the appearing of Jesus Christ; whom having not seen, ye love; in whom, though now ye see him not, yet believing, ye rejoice with joy unspeakable and full of glory; receiving the end of your faith, even the salvation of your souls."

CHAPTER II

THE SEAT OF AUTHORITY IN RELIGION

M. Sabatier seems to have made a false antithesis in the title of his book: *Religions of Authority and the Religion of the Spirit.* For if he accepts his religious feelings, which are the subjective side of the religion of the spirit, as the basis of his religious beliefs, he thereby concedes the authority of his feelings. If, however, he appeals to Reason in support of his decision, then Reason as authenticating the feelings, is the ultimate religious authority. And if again Reason should decline to adjudicate in respect to the feelings on the ground that in such matters she could not be trusted, the appellant would be confronted with a contradiction: for whether he trusted her, in spite of her claim that she could not be trusted, or believed her when she said she could not be trusted, he would in either case be trusting her. But this only shows how hard it is to impeach Reason when it is at the bar of Reason that the case against her has to be tried. As Kirkman said many years ago, you cannot carve your goose and carve your carving knife at the same time.[1]

The subject of this lecture is "The Seat of Au-

---

[1] *Philosophy without Assumptions,* 194.

thority in Religion," and as Reason is one of the claimants for this position, the other two being the Church and the Bible, let us enter at once upon the consideration of her claims.

i

THE REASON

There are no difficulties in revealed religion which have not also appeared in natural religion. This substantially was the thesis which Bishop Butler so ably defended in his immortal *Analogy*. Many apologetic writings have been produced since, but none has displaced Butler's from the high position accorded it on its first appearance. Designed to convince deists and show that believing as they did in God there was no reason why they should not believe also in the Christian revelation, it is said to have had the opposite effect upon some minds: the difficulties exhibited in connection with religion, natural and revealed, leading them, it is said, to drop both. A similar criticism has been made regarding two other treatises which have since appeared in English apologetics.

A little more than half a century ago Dean Mansel published his Bampton Lectures on *The Limits of Religious Thought* based upon the idea that since the same difficulties appear alike in philosophy and religion it is proper to assume that there are limits to religious thought, which, on the one hand, make a system of rational theology impossible, and on the other hand impose on us the necessity of believing on the authority of revelation what transcends the power of reason to comprehend. To this statement there can hardly be any objection, but in the development of his thesis Mansel exposed himself to much just criticism, with the result that what was intended as a defence of Christianity has been generally regarded as a leading contribution to agnosticism. There was truth, however, on both sides of this famous controversy.

Almost forty years ago Mr. A. J. Balfour (now the Earl of Balfour) published his *Defence of Philosophic Doubt,* the object of which was to show that science had no right to ridicule theology, since the one had quite as little philosophical support as the other. Nothing that Lord Balfour has since written exceeds in logical acumen and clever criticism his earlier book. I will not say that I did not enjoy the warning to those who live in the glass house of science not to throw stones at the theologians; but I did not like the implication that the latter were living in a residence equally fragile; nor did I feel disposed to retire from the active business of thinking, in order to live in indolent comfort on a pension of faith. A recent reading of the *Defence of Philosophic Doubt* does not change my estimate of its ability, nor my dissatisfaction with its conclusions.

I do not feel that I have sufficiently thought

through the author's position to do more than raise the modest query whether Lord Balfour's attitude in his Gifford Lectures is quite the same as it was in his *Philosophic Doubt;* whether in fact he does not now assign more value to the argument from "general consent" than he did forty years ago (I refer here, of course, to the fine use he makes of our "familiar beliefs") ; and whether he has not a more lenient feeling towards transcendental deduction than he once had. "All transcendental arguments," he says in the earlier work, "convince by threats." This is not necessarily a disparagement of this mode of argument and cannot be so intended. "Allow my conclusion, they say, or I will prove to you that you must surrender one of your most cherished beliefs."[2] It is precisely this form of argument that Lord Balfour uses at the close of his second course of Gifford Lectures, for he says the conclusion is "that for certain difficulties attaching to the familiar beliefs by which we live, the true remedy is to be found in Theism. In other words, Divine guidance must be postulated if we are to maintain the three great values—knowledge, love, and beauty."[3] Concerning the cogency of this argument there is no room for doubt, and I will take the liberty to say that in these Lectures Lord Balfour has done invaluable service to the cause of theism.

[2] *A Defence of Philosophic Doubt,* 114.
[3] *Theism and Thought,* 242.

1. REASON AND FAITH. Turning now to the claim of Reason to be placed in a seat of authority in religious matters, it seems clear that we cannot place the entire content of religion to the exclusive credit of either Reason or Faith; for there are some things that we cannot help believing, and others which we have no right to believe without the support of adequate evidence. This, of course, is just as true of science as it is of religion.

Leverrier predicted the appearance of the planet Neptune, taking as his postulate the uniformity of nature which, as can be readily shown, is either an *a priori* belief or an unverified hypothesis. Then by a process of mathematical reasoning he made his prediction, which was verified when the new planet swam into the ken of the observer. *Credo ut intelligam* is therefore the course of thought in inductive reasoning. This famous motto represents also the way in which most men acquire information. They accept without inquiry the general stock of human knowledge. They believe in the germ theory of disease, consent to vaccination, submit to the advice of counsel in legal matters, adopt the party cry of their political leaders, and assent to the tenets of their Church, without pretending to examine the reason for the faith that is in them. They say 'We wish to know what is going on in the world of science or politics; we wish to be guided wisely in matters of conduct and religious belief; and we seek information from those who are competent to give it.' Accordingly they read the daily papers, glance at the reviews, and listen to the conversation of men who are supposed to know. It is true that the information they receive is often misinformation. It is not uncommon for them to be misled by some ignorant but infatuated disciple of a novel idea, and that at best they are following opinions which they are incompetent to submit to critical tests. After various refractions and reflections the ray of light reaches them a little less clear than they could wish but still clear enough for practical purposes. But what else can they do? They wish to know, and therefore must believe those whom they regard as competent informers. Their motto is *Credo ut intelligam.*

Mr. McTaggart tells us[4] that we have no right to believe in dogmas that we have not investigated. And the worst of it is, he makes this assertion about religious beliefs, which more than all others are important. This is most unfortunate; for if it be a sound position it would limit religious belief to a few scientists, philosophers and theologians, and deprive the plain man of the comfort he finds in his religion. And moreover, since it is not uncommon for philosophers and scientific men to take very little interest in religion, Mr. McTaggart while conferring the franchise of faith upon men who do not value it, would disallow it to the great

---

[4] *Some Dogmas of Religion*, Section 242. Cf. W. K. Clifford, "The Ethics of Belief," in *Lectures and Essays*, II.

mass of people who have a special interest therein.

But Mr. McTaggart is altogether wrong in his contention. His plan would condemn the great mass of men to outer darkness and confine all knowledge to a few specialists, each of whom would know his own department, but would be in total ignorance of what his co-workers in other specialties know. Men of light and leading might accept the compliment of being the only ones who knew, but even they would not like to be denied the right of intercommunication with each other. Again we must say, that in spite of the plausible qualifications of his position, Mr. McTaggart errs. It is not only right but necessary for us to believe on the testimony of others. Faith is a labour-saving device. Faith is the dividend we receive as shareholders in a joint-stock company formed for the increase and diffusion of human knowledge. Faith is the earliest form of profit-sharing in the world's use of intellectual capital.

2. REASON AND KNOWLEDGE. To believe without knowing the reasons is a very different thing from believing without there being any reasons. For a reason is in the nature of a premise of an argument. It is that back to which we go in support of a statement. You cannot go behind the statement that the whole is greater than its part. With regard, however, to most of our beliefs we can get behind them, and this is what we do when we give reasons for a belief. So we have men who

read, think, and discover the grounds on which the common beliefs of mankind are held; men who give themselves to scientific research and add to the sum total of human knowledge; men who occupy themselves with the sources of knowledge and who confirm or modify accepted opinions in the sphere of history. These men will say, 'We wish to enlarge our list of beliefs, wish to hold a firmer grip on what we already believe, wish to investigate phenomena in a way so searching that it may end in discrediting an old belief and putting a new conviction on its feet.' The motto for men of this class is *Intelligo ut credam*. Men of this sort are like the men of Sychar, who said to the woman of Samaria, "Now we believe, not because of thy saying; for we have heard him ourselves, and know that this is indeed the Christ the Saviour of the world."

But we must not suppose that because truth will produce faith, therefore faith will produce truth. Whatever the truth may be, there is a reason for it unless it is an ultimate and necessary truth. The plain man does not see this; and so he easily surrenders himself to attractive novelties, to unjustifiable beliefs and to forms of religion which have no semblance of evidence in their support. Starting with the fundamental principles of identity, contradiction and excluded middle, possessed of the empty categories which condition the possibility of experience, and following the rubrics of deductive logic, men have constructed great systems of philosophy which are not necessarily true because they are logically coherent; for while inconsistency is a note of error, consistency is not a guarantee of truth.

Nor can we give rein to our imagination and proclaim that we have discovered truth because we have used the categories, unless we make it clear to begin with that we are intentionally exercising our imagination. We cannot make possibility a test of truth except in regard to the coherency of a story. We have but five gateways of knowledge, but how many senses a man may have in the next world we do not know. And so stories have been written on the supposition that a man in another life may have one hundred senses and therefore that the man with only seventy would find himself uncomfortably restricted.[5] So men at the present day are writing books which contravene the known conditions of experience; and it is quite conceivable that men may write philosophy under an impulse similar to that which leads men to write stories. Eager to say something new, conquered by the force of a fresh idea, driven by a desire to show that accepted truths are vulnerable, they find scope for invention in framing new hypotheses. They act as a man would who, making the plan of a story, seeks to find a new set of circumstances to envisage

---

[5] See Fraser's *Berkeley*, in "Blackwood's Philosophical Classics," 80.

a bizarre theory of conduct, and to portray the hero under conditions which have never yet been made the theme of fiction. This, of course, is quite allowable when the motive is to please. But it is a very different thing when men write epistemological romances and so give to their airy nothings a local habitation and a name. Of not a little contemporary philosophical thought it may be said that it shows cleverness, but is nevertheless open to criticism, because it goes forth in the name of truth, and by its pretensions serves to deceive the unwary. It is so easy sometimes by throwing a stone into the placid stream of conviction to persuade men that the ripples it makes are the truth they are seeking.

Nor will it do to say that the search for truth is limited to the sphere of experience, for much of our knowledge does transcend experience. We have a confident belief amounting to knowledge that sodium exists in the sun, the lines of the spectrum made by the sodium of experience corresponding to similar lines in the solar spectrum. That the inference is sound, no one calls in question; but for the verification of the hypothesis we must wait till a bit of sodium comes down from the sun. Our knowledge, in other words, is in the terms of probability. More and more, I am told, men are coming to believe in what is called the four dimensional continuum. Yet it, too, transcends experience. We cannot conceive of it, we cannot make a working model of it, for we should have to use materials of three dimensions; but if mathematical reasoning should result in placing it on a basis of strong probability it would take its place as an article of scientific faith.

On the other hand, we cannot accept as true a proposition that destroys truth, or admit into the list of things known what would overthrow the possibility of knowledge. If men choose to accept a theory which contradicts itself they must be allowed to do so, but they must face the opposition which will inevitably follow; and this is the indictment that is being brought against certain forms of science and philosophy at the present day. When, for example, we are told that "Truth is our most general form of human liking,"[6] we are told by implication that if we do not like it we may leave it alone. This pragmatic theory of truth cuts as closely to the roots of knowledge as we can well imagine; and once we are convinced that truth is a mere matter of subjectivity, the search for truth will be the idlest of all employments.

When, again, we are told that our *a priori* beliefs—the certitudes with which we have been set up in the business of thinking—resolve themselves into certain arrangements of material particles which through a long succession of ages have in

---

[6] David W. Prall, "The Present Status of the Theory of Value," *University of California Publications in Philosophy,* IV, 94.

all their changes been predetermined, we need no argument to show that the science which teaches this is wrong. For it means that the entire scheme of interconnectedness which we call the world is nothing short of a mechanism; that Leonardo da Vinci's "Last Supper" is as mechanical as the cheapest chromo; that the finest symphony is as much the result of a mechanical arrangement of material atoms as the "record" of a Victrola; that the writings of Plato and Aristotle are the outcome of centuries of pre-arranged material atoms; and that what we call the knowledge of all this, is itself a certain state of material particles to which we give the name of "thought." A theory which so obviously refutes itself and destroys the meaning of thought, inference, belief, proof, and knowledge, needs no other and can have no better refutation than the statement of the case. A mindless world can neither make arguments nor accept proofs.

This is the issue to-day between science and religion. But to say that this is the doctrine of evolution is a very different thing, and all depends on the question whether the evolutionary process is to be explained in the terms of matter alone, of mind alone, or of both matter and mind. Whether it is the duty of evolutionists to clear their skirts of the taint of materialism, or the duty of the critic of the evolutionists to be sure of his facts before framing his indictment against a large class of respectable thinkers, is a matter which the parties in controversy must settle among themselves.

3. REASON AND RELIGION. Whether this or that religion is true, and whether any religion is true, are questions to be settled on the evidence. But the presence of religion as a large factor in human life raises at least a strong presumption in favour of some form of religious faith. If, then, in view of the various forms of religious belief to be found in the world, a man chooses to say that one religion is as good as another, it is probably because of the elements in each which are common to all; though why we should consider these common beliefs rather than the differences between religions, it is hard to say. For, the differences existing, Reason has no right to say that the value of any religion consists in what it has in common with all other religions; and if a claim for exceptional treatment is made for any one religion, Reason as an impartial judge is bound to give heed to the reasons urged for this exceptional religion. On the assumption, however, that all religions are of equal value, Reason may try to find the elements held in solution by all of them, and this would result in a philosophy of religion. Inasmuch, however, as differences have also a right to be considered, Reason may be usefully employed in reducing the religions of the world to a statement of their contents with particular reference to their differences and

their points of agreement. The result of this undertaking would be a science of religion.

The outcome of this investigation may result in a decision favorable to Christianity on the basis of the exceptional evidence in its support. But before considering that matter, let us suppose that the decision of reason is in favor of Christianity to the exclusion of other religions. Will anyone kindly tell me why Christian men and men of no religion, who have not studied the subject, should be so much more interested in other religions than in Christianity? Valuable the knowledge of the other religions undoubtedly is to the missionary who is anxious to find a point of contact between himself and the heathen world, valuable for comparative purposes to show wherein Christianity excels all other religions, valuable too as showing that these religions were providential anticipations of a wider and more important truth; but is this interest in Buddhism, for example, of such moment that men living in a Christian country should be all the time sounding its praises, with the implication of a corresponding disparagement of the Christian faith?

I confess that the cleverness with which some men speak of Confucianism, Buddhism, Brahminism, and Zoroastrianism, compared with the slight appreciation which they seem to have of Christianity, reminds me of a conductor, charged with the responsibility for an express train from New York to Chicago, who had made a comparative study of railway time-tables at the expense of an intimate acquaintance with the schedule of his own road. At half past eleven in the forenoon he informs his astonished passengers that in ten minutes the New Orleans express will arrive in Chicago; a little later and to the passengers in another car, he says that the Denver express is due in the same city at twenty minutes past one. But meanwhile he has forgotten his "wired" orders to take a siding twenty miles out from Chicago because there was a wreck on the main line. How much better it would have been for him and his passengers had he known less about other roads and attended exclusively to his own business!

4. REASON AND CHRISTIANITY. Assuming now that the Bible is a record of supernatural revelation, it is the office of Reason to interpret the Scriptures. This is not as simple a matter as it may seem; and those who think that a vast amount of learning has been uselessly employed in the interpretation of a book which the plain man can read for himself, have but a dim conception of the amount of inductive study which has been devoted to the interpretation of the Scriptures. Without going into argument, we may safely assume that centuries of learned debate over the meaning of the Bible would not have been necessary if its meaning were so obviously on its surface that the wayfaring man need not err therein. More than he is aware, undoubtedly, the unlearned reader is in-

debted to the controversies which he treats with such scant consideration for his ability to see upon the face of Scripture the meaning which he reads into it; for as a rule he has grown into his place as an independent student of the Bible after a long process of training in a Christian home and under the instruction of Christian teachers. Let us, then, make proper acknowledgment of the great work which Reason has done in the unfolding of the meaning of the Bible through the representative theologians of the Church in all ages.

But we have now to consider another question, and that is whether in the light of scholarly and scientific investigation we can continue to trust the Scriptures as the rule of faith and practice. A man may say that this debate has no interest for him, for the Bible is its own witness and needs no defence. Believing as I do in the supreme authority of the Bible, I have no fear that its unlearned reader will suffer any loss by declining to take part in a controversy; for when an action of ouster is begun against the heirs of an estate, those who take no part in the litigation will benefit as much by a favorable decision of the Court as those who bear the expenses of the suit. But this does not prove that the suit ought not to have been defended. Aside, however, from controversy, it is clear that Reason must give a decision and let us know which of the world's sacred books ought to be taken as a rule of faith; or, left to their own unreasoned choice, men may select the Vedas, the Shastras, or the writings of Confucius; or yet again, as some are now doing, the Koran, the book of the Mormon faith, or of Mrs. Eddy.

But the question arises, what shall we do in the great issue raised by philosophy, science and history against the truth of Christianity? Some say 'Make no reply. The motive of the attack is hostility to Christianity, and the attack itself is based on a foregone conclusion.' There is some force in this, and obviously it would be a pity if the active energies of the Church were crippled by controversy. Shall the Church reply, 'Acting by advice of counsel I have nothing to say?' Shall she risk the charge of cowardice? Can she avoid saying something? When the great case of Christianity *v.* Science, Philosophy, and History is tried, can she give evidence in direct testimony and refuse to be cross-examined? Can she expect the case to be settled on *ex parte* testimony, in defiance of the maxim *Audi alteram partem?* Should she let it go by default and be satisfied with the record of the Court that the defendant did not appear? It may be an open question in the debate between Christianity and its opponents who is plaintiff and who is defendant. On this nothing need here be said, but of this I am confident, that when through her counsel Christianity is plaintiff, it is of the utmost importance that her legal advisers do not raise a false issue.

The Christian apologete is sometimes blamed because he shows the ardor of the advocate rather than the dispassionate calmness of the judge. But this is surely an unjust criticism. Do you find fault with the zeal of the man who enters into litigation for the protection of his property when an attempt is made to turn him out of his home? I think we must admit that the frigid logic of the student who seeks the solution of a problem in mathematical physics would ill become a defender of the faith.

It is also said that the apologete is arguing "in chains," since whatever the facts may be his conclusions are made for him in advance.

Bishop Gore has dwelt very satisfactorily with this matter in his *The Holy Spirit and the Church,* and I have referred to the subject in a sermon preached at the opening of the centennial celebration of Princeton Theological Seminary in 1912, from which the following words are taken.

> There is a certain amount of force in this criticism which I do not overlook, though I think that far too much is made of it. But we must be careful, in acknowledging the element of justice in the criticism, not to fall into the very common mistake of supposing that a man's position as an advocate operates to the prejudice of his full knowledge of the facts. Biased he may be, but ignorant he

if, instead of hypostatizing an abstraction, whether it be called "life" or "activity," he found in the living God an answer to reason's question. And when we get to the bottom of these conflicting answers to this question, what an unacknowledged witness they bear to the truth that we cannot flee from God's presence. The Psalmist got at the root of all philosophy when he said: "If I ascend up to heaven thou art there, if I make my bed in hell, behold thou art there; if I take the wings of the morning and flee to the uttermost parts of the earth, even there shall thy hand find me and thy right hand uphold me."

There is a sense in which individuated reason is identical with the various phases of intellectual effort and endowment. There is also a sense in which Reason in her ultimate averments may be regarded as the common dotation of our race. So considered, in this universal aspect, how wonderful and how widely spread is her witness to things unseen. If amid the strife of tongues we would only listen to her undertones we should find that she is whispering God's message in our ear. How persistently she strives to soar above the mists and clouds of earth to seek the sunlight of God's favour; and though she sometimes falls with broken wing, let us not laugh at her lameness but rather see even in her failure another witness to the truth that "God has set eternity in our hearts."

ii

THE CHURCH

If, in the tomb of Tutankhamen there were found historical records showing that, long before the Christian era, there was a man who claimed to have a revelation from God, who lived a blameless life, taught a faultless morality and moreover did wonderful works; that he gathered disciples around him and founded a society which propagated his teaching: would the discovery of those documents be sufficient to revive that religion and assure its successful propagation in the twentieth century? I imagine not. For if this religion were what it claimed to be, why did it die? and dying, how could we set up anew the conditions necessary to restore it? This only serves to show that one of the strongest arguments in support of Christianity is its uninterrupted stream of history, and the blessings of civilization that follow and proceed from it. There is, then, this to be said for Christianity, whatever the form may be in which it manifests itself, which would make it worth while to examine its claims.

Not long ago considerable interest was awakened by the discovery of what is known as "the Antioch cup," which by many is regarded as the same from which the Saviour drank, which he handed to his beloved disciple who leaned on his bosom, and of which they all partook on the night of his be-

[117]

trayal. If this belief were confirmed, we can imagine what interest it would awaken, what pilgrimages would be made to see it, and what efforts there would be to secure the honour of being its custodian. We can understand, then, the interest men have in relics and how superstition and an ignorant credulity can make them "aids to faith." For we have only to realize that an ordinary heirloom will take us back across the threshold of two or three centuries and fill us with emotions bordering on reverence, in order to understand this feature in Christianity; so that whatever be our view as to the history of the Church, there is something amounting, at least, to a very strong presumption favourable to her claims in the fact that we have not only historic documents, but a sacramental service dating from the first century of our era, together with an unbroken history, to support the Christian faith. Whatever differences exist among Christians, and however much we may feel ourselves separated from, let us say, the Roman Catholic Church, we cannot escape from the fact that it was through her we came into possession of a rich treasure of historical tradition. The question, what is the Church, however, is one of great moment.

1. THE MEANING OF THE CHURCH. The Roman Catholic says that the Church consists of those who partake of the same sacraments, are under lawful pastors and teachers, and in obedience

to the Pope. We may say, and do say, that the
Church so defined is very different from the Church
as it existed in the days of the Apostles. So those
argue who say that nothing corresponding to the
Roman conception of the Church existed in the
first century of our era. Accordingly, the Reformed theologians, under the leadership of Calvin, undertook to reconstruct the organization of
the Church on a Presbyterian basis claiming, as I
think very properly, that a system of diocesan episcopacy is not to be found in the New Testament;
the words 'bishop' and 'presbyter' being convert-
ible terms. I feel confident that the reasoning on
this subject is correct. But when Protestantism
broke away from the Roman obedience and set up
the Anglican Church, the doctrine of its episcopal
constitution was not changed and by a certain section of that Church was and still is maintained to
be a note of the true Church. How, then, does
the Anglican Church escape the charge of schism?
Does it hold that the Roman Catholic Church is in
schism and that the Anglican is the true Church?
That, to say the least, would be a difficult proposition to prove. Well, then, if it be conceded that
the Anglican Church is part of the Church Catholic
on the ground that it keeps episcopacy and the
apostolic succession, the question arises, How small
may a fragment be and still remain a part of the
true Church? The logic of Anglicanism would

seem to be not *ubi Petrus,* but *ubi episcopus, ibi ecclesia.*

Presbyterians, however, were not the only ones who disputed the claims of apostolic succession; for there were those who said: 'If you are going to base your conception of the Church on the New Testament, a great deal can be said for the independence of each congregation.' And so it came to pass that we have three competing forms of Church government, each claiming for itself *jure divino* authority: Episcopacy, Presbyterianism, and Congregationalism. I have no eager interest in these debates, because I am far from being persuaded that any particular form of Church government can claim the exclusive authority of existing by Divine right. The exigencies of the early Church may easily have led to the development of a monarchical form of Church government. Human ambition may have aided this development, and what led to the establishment of diocesan episcopacy may have led to that of archbishoprics, patriarchates, and the papacy. Nor need there be in this highest and latest form of development any necessary repudiation of any inherent principle of Christianity. The logic which justifies the first step will justify the last.

Meanwhile, to return for a moment to the Anglican conception of Church government, Anglicans are not agreed among themselves. In the Preface to the sixth edition of his *Philippians,*

Bishop Lightfoot qualified the 'concessions' made in the *Dissertation on the Christian Ministry*, which was not unnaturally regarded as having established the position that originally bishop and presbyter were synonymous terms. Bishop Gore, while admitting that diocesan episcopacy cannot be found in the New Testament, is a strong believer in the sacerdotal idea of the ministry and an ardent advocate of episcopacy and apostolic succession.[7] Dr. Headlam points out that the term Apostolic Succession is used with different significations and says that in the sense that "for a valid ministry and the due performance of the Sacraments, this succession and transmission by ordination is necessary," this theory, so far as he is able to judge, "was not held at all in the early Church."[8] Dr. Rawlinson, no doubt correctly, sums up the present situation when he says that in so far as "the case has been represented as depending on the alleged form assumed by the ministry in the first age of the Church," "the resultant position is one of stale-mate."[9] All of us will agree that episcopacy made its appearance at a very early period in the Church after the close of the New Testament canon and that it has proved to be a very efficient form of Church government.

But this position gives rise to another question,

---

[7] See his *The Holy Spirit in the Church* and *The Church and the Ministry*.

[8] *The Doctrine of the Church and Christian Reunion*, 124–8.

[9] A. E. J. Rawlinson, "The Principle of Authority," *Foundations*, 382–3.

and that is, whether organization is of the essence of the Church. I do not mean by this question to inquire whether organization is desirable or expedient, but whether it is essential to the existence of the Church. For if it is of the essence of the Church that it be organized, then the question what this organization is becomes a matter of the highest importance. I am one of those who do not believe that organization is of the essence of the Church, and therefore I make no obstinate plea in favour of Presbyterianism in opposition to Episcopacy. When a meeting is called for the discussion of a public question and the assembly is ready for business, the appointment of a chairman and a secretary is a wise precaution. But the meeting consists of the same individuals after the organization as before, and if in its unorganized condition it could express its wish to the extent of making an organization, had it seen fit, it could have gone on doing so without an organization. I therefore agree with those who say that the Church consists of all those 'who profess the true religion together with their children'; or with those—to use another formula—who say that it consists of all 'who profess and call themselves Christians,' whether they believe in this, that, or the other form of organization or in no organization at all.

2. THE FUNCTION OF THE CHURCH. As in regard to the nature of the Church, so in respect to its functions, there is great difference of opin-

ion among Christians, which is perhaps sufficiently indicated in what follows.

(1) *To teach.* This will be accepted by Church organizations of every name. Our Lord's command to his disciples was to "teach all nations." The evangelization of the world proceeds upon the supposition that the Church was charged with a message. As a natural result of this the Church formulated the message in certain beliefs or doctrinal statements, and while differences of belief are the occasion for the existence of different organizations, there is a core of Christian doctrine representing a consensus of Christian faith which these Christian denominations consider it their duty to preach.

(2) *To be a channel of grace.* There is a sense in which the great mass of Christian people accept this view. The Church is an agency for promoting religion among its members and for the spread of the Gospel in heathen lands. This common agreement calls for no discussion. But by a very large portion of Christendom the Church is regarded as the channel by which the blessings of Christianity are communicated. According to this view the sacraments—except baptism—can be administered only by a priest, and the priest must be ordained by a bishop, the latter being—in an unbroken line—a successor of the Apostles. Those who hold this view are quite within their rights when they carry their conviction to its logical con-

sequences. A great deal of bigotry and interdenominational ill-feeling is due to the fact that men will not see that a priest of the Roman or Anglican Church is in duty bound to be true to his deepest convictions. Let us then understand the position of the Roman Catholic Church and of some in the Anglican communion. The Church is regarded as an organism and sustains a relation to the Holy Spirit like that of the body to the soul. There are passages of Scripture which, taken by themselves, seem to sustain this position. You may as well expect your little finger to maintain a separate life after it is amputated as to suppose that one can be the recipient of divine grace after he is separated from the Church. It is easy to see, therefore, what, to a Roman Catholic, excommunication means. How closely a Roman Catholic or an Anglo-Catholic follows this premise to its conclusion, I do not know; but I have no fault to find if he feels himself forced to say *Extra ecclesiam nulla salus*.

This view of the Church is unmistakably taught by Dr. Gore in his recent book *The Holy Spirit and the Church*. One cannot help admiring the attitude of the former Bishop of Oxford in this volume. It is in close keeping with the position he took in *Lux Mundi* upwards of thirty years ago and fully sustains his own estimate of himself as being at once a Catholic and a free thinker. In the *Lux Mundi* essay I saw on its appearance that much as he might wish it, the author could not be indifferent to the results of the higher criticism without endangering his view of the Church. In the present volume he holds apparently a purposely mediating position between the Roman Catholic and the Anglican Modernist. Just as far as he can, he goes with the Roman Catholic in matters of *cultus* and tradition—conceding reverence for relics, adoration of the Virgin Mary and a reverent regard for tradition; but with an outspoken difference with respect to the authority of the Scriptures. It must be conceded that Dr. Gore has proved himself to be a clever helmsman in steering safely between the Scylla of ultra-Montanism and the Charybdis of Father Tyrrelism, and it may be said of him that without any sacrifice of his convictions he has made an attempt to be all things to all men if by any means he may save some.

But the Church regarded as the channel of grace must be also considered in connection with current movements looking toward the reunion of Christendom. It is easy to see the difficulties of such reunion on the terms of the Lambeth Conference and certain proposed modifications of them, no matter how much we admire the fine Christian spirit that underlies them. The reunion of Christendom would have but little meaning to Anglo-Catholics unless it contemplated a reunion with Rome. What changes may take place in the liberalizing of Roman Catholic opinion we cannot say. At present there is no indication that the Vatican will alter its policy or abandon its proud boast of *semper eadem*, and there seems to be but little prospect of a union between Roman and Anglo-Catholics except by a return to the Roman obedience. Such a movement, however, if attempted by the Church of England would arouse a Protestant sentiment, political and religious, which would in all probability overthrow the established Church. More important, however, and perhaps more easily accomplished, would be the return of the Nonconformist Churches to the Church of their fathers. But the ministers of these Free Churches would not like to pass a vote of want of confidence in their own 'orders' by accepting Episcopal ordination. There are indications, however, that this would not be required of them. But these are matters which are outside my province.

Let us consider, then, the union of non-Episcopal denominations among themselves. The idea is gaining ground that denominationalism has served its purpose and the demand is being made for a comprehensive Church, a Church which will be based on a shorter creed with a wide toleration of the differences that characterize the several sects. These Churches hold no organic theory akin to that of the Anglican and Roman Catholic Churches. The logic of Protestantism is individualism. Its Churches are organizations and not organisms. Let us conceive of the Presbyterian churches, for example, as consisting of so many grains of sand put into a bag called the Presbyterian Church. Under the same simile let us think of the Methodists, Baptists, and other denominations. And now let us suppose that a union of these and other denominations is effected by pouring the contents of these little bags of sand into a larger one to which a new name is given. Does the larger denomination formed by this. union acquire as the result of the union the character of an organism? Can you say of the greater organization thus effected that it is a channel of grace in a sense that was not true of each Church before the union was accomplished? I think not. Is there anything in this larger denomination so corresponding to the idea of an organism that to break away from it would involve the loss of grace through separation from what is the channel of grace? Nothing at all. Is there in the effecting of the union anything which would ensure its permanence, protect it against disruption, and in any way make up for the severing of old ties and the breaking up of old associations? Nothing.

But certain results would follow. You would not have five churches in a town which can ill afford to support more than one. There would be an economic gain. It would be a money-saving enterprise, though that would not be all. But the union would mean that certain doctrines believed to be taught in Scripture would no longer be regarded as worth contending for. The idea of a witness-bearing Church would cease to have any special significance. In other words, such a union would be the most palpable exhibition of a general conviction that what was once thought worth contending for is no longer worth what it costs. The merger of the Churches would mean but little more than the merger of two banks, where by joint capitalization, increased volume of business and reduced overhead charges, larger dividends would fall to the lot of the shareholders. The merger of non-Episcopal Churches would be a merger of organizations and would lack the distinction of an organism.[10]

(3) *To keep the deposit of faith.* It seems that a certain 'deposit' was entrusted to the keeping of the Church. We should like to know what it was and whether it is still in safe keeping. The word "deposit' has a connotation to the layman different from that given to it by theologians, though its meaning will be plain enough before I finish. But I must use the commercial meaning of the word to help me in this theological exposition. I can remember when there was only one Trust Company in New York, but there are several of them now; and there are several Trust Companies claiming to have possession of at least a portion of

[10] For some fine thoughts on the Reunion of Christendom, see Dr. (now Bishop) Headlam's volume and Dr. Rawlinson's essay, referred to above.

this 'deposit of faith.' Some feel that they have special charge of some of the deposit. The Presbyterians, for example, seem to have the "decrees of God" in their special keeping, and the sacrament of baptism is in still other hands. But most of these companies are of comparatively recent date. John Calvin got in pretty early with his, as we all know. Then again, there is the Church of England whose position is not easy to define. Blunt argues at length that she has a continuous and unbroken history, that she did not cease to be Catholic at the Reformation, and that in becoming "independent of the Roman See" she was not "in any way separated from communion with it."[11]

Bishop Short says that the Church of England must be dated from the divorce of Henry VIII from Catharine of Arragon, that it became entirely Protestant under Edward VI, and after varying fortunes under Mary, Elizabeth and succeeding monarchs, became at the time of the Revolution in 1688, "as it has continued ever since, a paid and authorized church establishment."[12] This historical question, however, I do not discuss.

Then, again, some of the modern companies are offshoots from the Anglican Trust Company: the Independents for example who went out in 1662 —not exactly because they wanted to go, however; and the Wesleyans who entered upon their separ-

[11] The Reformation of the Church of England, 255.
[12] History of the Church of England, 488-90.

interest. Even so prosaic a profession as the law recognizes this in the maxim *Haeret in litera, haeret in cortice.* You read the Bible, and if your mind is active it suggests thoughts to you which are not in the text, but are not without their value on that account. For the way that thought begets thought is one of the most wonderful things in experience. A writer, for example, is doing his work, and as he broods two lines of verse creep out of memory-cells and beget a fresh metaphor. Comes then a flash of thought, or a flush of feeling, and there falls a glint of golden light upon his page. The power to see things in the Bible which grammar does not teach makes all the difference between poetry and prose; and to miss what the Bible suggests through devotion to what it states is to miss the opportunity of learning valuable lessons. On the other hand, to seize on what it suggests to the neglect of what it states is fruitful of serious error.

You remember the passage in Lecky's *History of Rationalism,*[13] beginning with the words "The world is governed by its ideals." He goes on to tell us how the place of the Virgin Mary in the thought of Medieval Christendom has shaped the history of chivalry. We can well imagine that some cloistered monk thinking about the Virgin would say, 'It is impossible that she should have

[13] W. E. H. Lecky, *History of the Rise and Influence of the Spirit of Rationalism in Europe,* I, 225.

been born with the taint of original sin; it is impossible that a being so pure should see death.' And so at length we have the doctrine of the Immaculate Conception of the Virgin, and her Bodily Assumption. And thus they turn what should have been a private possession into a mechanical dogma, with the result that what would have been beautiful for what it was, becomes grotesque by what they made of it.

The Roman Catholic attitude, however, means something more than sentiment and perhaps resembles that of the man who feels that the Constitution of the United States while suited for the time in which it was made, does not meet the exigencies of Government at the present day, and therefore needs a very liberal construction or frequent amendment. The Church being the organ of the Holy Ghost, the Roman Catholic feels that she may add to the content of Revelation. This being his position we ask, "By what right do you presume to add to the Revelation of God?" And the answer would be that the Church is infallible, and therefore has the right to speak in the present tense. See, then, the advantage that the Church can claim. We depend on the Bible with its differences of interpretation and its difficulties of criticism, but the Church has the right to declare through a General Council or the Pope what is *de fide* now. How does he defend this position? In part at least by appeal to the Scriptures. And

he cites the passages which are familiar to us all.
But there are two questions he has never answered
satisfactorily: Do these promises to the Church
imply the Church's infallibility? And if they do,
does the Church to which these promises are made
mean the Roman Catholic Church?

The doctrine of the infallibility of the Church
is a very convenient belief I grant, and not absurd
either. The only question is whether there is evidence in support of it. Convenient, of course; for,
consider. The Protestant asks in regard to a
mooted doctrine, What do the Scriptures teach?
The Anglican asks the same question, but he also
asks, What do the Church Fathers say? What has
been the faith of the Church from the beginning?
It was not strange then, that a certain clergyman
who left the Anglican Church and went over to
Rome, said to his quondam brethren, 'Your religion is salvation by scholarship alone.' The Roman
Catholic, however, cannot get away from the Bible
as the ultimate authority so long as he appeals to
the Bible in support of the infallibility of the
Church. Suppose, then, that a young man is seeking light on this subject and wishes first of all to
know where the true Church is to be found. To
what disinterested authority can he appeal? To
no other than the Bible. How shall he interpret
the Bible? Shall he ask a Protestant minister? 'No,'
he says, 'for he would be biased.' Shall he ask a
Roman Catholic priest? 'No, for I know what his

answer would be. I must read the Bible for myself in the light of my own reason.'

That is to say, in order to determine whether he should become a Protestant or become a Roman Catholic he must act on the principle that the Bible is the only rule of faith and in the exercise of the right of private judgment; which amounts to saying that a man has to be a Protestant in order to become a Catholic.[14] Granting, therefore, all that can be said in behalf of Reason and the Church, we cannot avoid the conclusion that the supreme authority in support of the content of Christianity is the Bible. Grant that it is the function of reason to consider the claims of the Bible to be a revelation from God by scrutinizing the evidence which accredits it; grant, too, that the New Testament was produced by the primitive Christian community and therefore that the Church antedated the Scriptures; it is still true that the Church gets the warrant for her faith and the programme of her action out of the Scriptures.

That the Roman Catholic Church is in serious error on some important questions admits of no doubt if the Scriptures are to be our guide. She teaches what is not taught in Scripture and misteaches some things that are taught there. There are, however, some palliating circumstances, as in her doctrine of the sacraments where five have been

---

[14] Cf. George Cornewall Lewis, *The Influence of Authority in Matters of Opinion*, 44.

added to the two instituted by Christ. But we have only to rationalize these five as Möhler did, or rather to desacramentalize them, to see that they are after all not such gross departures from primitive Christianity as at first sight they seem to be. Confirmation, for example—retained in the Lutheran and Anglican Churches, but not as a sacrament—is a very proper, solemn, and dignified method of introducing young persons into full communion with the Church. I have always heard, though I cannot put my hand upon the evidence for it, that Dr. Charles Hodge regretted that the Presbyterian Churches gave up this service, and I am in full accord with his sentiment. All Churches agree that marriage should be solemnized with the rites of the Church. Ordination is a solemn function in which a candidate for the ministry is set apart for the spiritual functions of his office. Penance as a sacrament is the natural outcome of 'confession' and the denial of the doctrine of justification by faith. If confession is made a duty it is liable to abuse, but if it is considered as a privilege it becomes a very different matter. I see no reason why those who are perplexed in respect to what they ought to do or have done, should not have the advice of a minister of the Gospel on some delicate questions of casuistry, without the risk of having a private matter made a topic of gossipy conversation. I have no doubt that ministers are called on more commonly than we suppose and that they regard it as one of the privileges of their office to aid in the solution of questions of conscience.

And last of all there is the sacrament of extreme unction, for which I have no plea to make and no analogy to offer save in the comforting visit of the Protestant minister to "the sick, the afflicted and the dying." Father Tyrrell, though he had abandoned the cardinal doctrines of his Church and of Christianity, craved extreme unction—and received it—when he came to die. I asked one who had been on intimate terms with him how it was that such a minor matter could have any interest for him in view of his apostacy from the Christian faith, and I was told in substance that it was due to the power of old associations and that his feeling was akin to that of one who craved what he would regard as decent burial.

I cannot think that the Roman Church puts all of these sacraments on the same level, nor does she, for baptism may be performed by a nurse to save a child from the peril of going unbaptized into the other world—a needless anxiety, as it seems to me—and the Lord's Supper has been lifted to the highest place in her ritual by a process of gradual exaggeration of its meaning. Yet these and other similar differences should not prevent the exercise of that mutual charity between Catholics and Protestants, which hopeth all things, believeth all things, endureth all things. And be these differences what they may, we should never forget that it was the Catholic Church which bore the Bible across the sea of centuries in "Peter's bark," and that whatever her faults may be she has never yet disowned her Lord nor cast doubt upon the doctrine of immortality.

iii

THE BIBLE

The third claimant for the seat of authority in religion is the Bible, and to that we must now give our attention. Two phases of this question present themselves; accordingly we must consider the Bible first as the judge of controversy, and secondly as a party to controversy.

1. THE BIBLE AS THE JUDGE OF CONTROVERSY. The attempt to reform the Church "in head and members" in the sixteenth century began with a presentation of the case to the adjudication of the Church. Failing there, the Reformers took a change of venue and made their appeal to the Bible as, in contradistinction to the claims of the Church, "the only infallible rule of faith and practice." It was claimed, however, that the Church was the only authorized interpreter of Scripture, but this was met by affirming the right of private judgment. This again was met by a reminder of the peril to which such an appeal gave rise, since the Church had the power of the keys; and then came the great affirmation of justification by faith. (This at least is the logical order and

I care little for chronological details.) Once convinced that the Scriptures are the seat of final authority, that the individual has the right to read the Bible for himself, and that salvation comes by the exercise of individual faith, the battle was won.

So were broken the chains that bound the consciences of men to the organization of the Church. So was launched the great principle of freedom which made possible the formation of free political institutions. So ended the business of brokerage in human souls. So were driven out the middlemen from the traffic in the wares of immortality, and so the individual began to transact the business of his soul alone with God. A great era in human history was thus ushered in by these three principles: the Bible the rule of faith, the right of private judgment, and justification by faith—representing the Reformation movement.

But suppose the emphasis had been put upon the right of private judgment. Then we should have lacked in the Reformed Churches the solidarity of conviction, the coöperative power of organization, and the cohesiveness of a common faith. The Reformers did not put the emphasis upon individual freedom but upon the authority of the Bible. They might have done that, however, without undertaking to expound the meaning of the Bible. In that case they would simply have put the Bible in place of the Church. And then just as the Roman Catholic says, 'I believe *explicitly* in the infallibility of the Church and therefore I believe *implicitly* in everything the Church teaches, whether I know what she teaches or not;' so the Protestant might have said, 'I believe explicitly in the inspiration of the Bible and therefore implicitly in all it says, whether I know what it says or not.' In both cases it would have been as if one put his medicine into a capsule, and swallowing the capsule swallowed the medicine too. But the Reformers did not stop with the affirmation of the Bible's authority. They sought to teach the meaning of the Bible; and accordingly as an early fruit of the Reformation we have the Augsburg Confession and the Formula of Concord, these being the two Lutheran Confessions of Faith; and a great many Reformed or Calvinistic Confessions, such as the first and second Helvetic Confessions, the Belgic Confession, the Heidelberg Catechism, the Thirty-Nine Articles, and the Westminster Confession of Faith. These ecclesiastical symbols might have been made longer, they might also have been made shorter. Subscription to them may be *in ipsissimis verbis* or with a tolerated divergence of view. In the case of the Church with which I am connected, it is clearly with the latter understanding. Two unions of the Presbyterian Church have made the recognition of a certain area of tolerated difference of opinion a moral obligation. But who is to decide what this area is?

This brings us to another issue, and one which

all Churches have to face; the issue, that is to say, between the letter and the spirit. I refer to the thought of to-day, the psychological climate in which we live, the change in relative values, and the temper of the time. These things must be considered when we pray for the peace of the Church. We need discernment not only in distinguishing between truth and error but also between the truths of greater and those of minor importance. But how is this area of tolerated divergence to be decided? Each denomination must settle that question for itself, but so far as it concerns the Church which I have the honor to serve, my belief is that it can only be decided by the General Assembly in a judicial case properly coming before it from the court of original jurisdiction. The General Assembly can impose no new terms of subscription; and as a commentary on, or an interpretation of *The Confession of Faith,* or an *in thesi* deliverance, would be equivalent to the making of a new term of subscription, such actions should not be taken as the basis of a judicial decision. In matters of this sort it is important to know not only what the express limitations of power are, but also the reasons for these limitations. We must first "visit and open the foundations and fountains of reason," as Bacon finely says[15] in the Case of the *Post-nati* of Scotland. In any Church we may always expect a conflict between the letter

[15] *Works,* Ellis and Spedding's ed., VII, 643.

Biblical account of the cosmogony and the Mosaic
origin of the Pentateuch. It has found in the different names for God evidence of a prevailing
polytheism with a gradual acceptance of a monotheistic faith; it has made reckless inferences based
on style and linguistic usage; it has dealt arbitrarily
with chronology; it has minimized the area of
predictive prophecy; it has tried to show that passages supposed to have Messianic reference were
intended only to apply to the political history of
Israel; and it has found in the moral lessons which
these Scriptures teach a satisfactory substitute for
the deep religious significance which they were
hitherto supposed to have.

(1) *Truth of the Bible.* It is not denied
that a plausible account of Old Testament history
can me made out by forced chronology, minute
linguistic appreciation, and *a priori* arguments
based on antisupernatural beliefs; the result being
that what was supposed to be intended as a preparation for Christianity is only the record of the
gradual development of a monotheistic faith. For it
must be remembered that the critics have a delicate
sense of literary values, such as was never known
by any student of English, or for that matter of
Greek literature, a sense so delicate that they have
been able to take a verse or two of the book of
Genesis and say what portion was due to the
Jahvist, what to the Elohist, and what to the Re-
dactor. With what accuracy, or rather what con-

fidence, this is done has been made visible to the eye of the unlearned reader in Haupt's polychrome Bible!

It is obvious that one who has not made Old Testament criticism the main study of his life cannot meet these critics on their own ground, and in maintaining an opposite opinion the unlearned must be guided by those who are competent to speak by reason of their highly specialized knowledge. Fortunately, however, there is no lack of men who with equal scholarship are able to defend the claims of the Old Testament Scriptures. Nor is it necessary for one to be a skilled orientalist in order to weigh the evidence and appraise the value of the arguments of those who take an active part on either side of this debate. A lawyer, for example, cannot be expected to be at once a banker, a broker, a merchant, and a master mariner in order to understand the merits of cases in these several lines of business which demand his professional attention. Those who are interested in this Old Testament problem will find an abundance of literature on both sides of the controversy.

But what I have particularly in mind is the fact that the battle ground of Christianity is the New Testament, for it is there that the evidence in support of the Christian faith is to be found. If Christianity cannot stand on the specific testimony of the New Testament, it is in vain to hope that the Old Testament can vindicate it; but on the other

hand, if the facts of the New Testament are true—
that is, are facts—then they confirm the claims of
the Old Testament. The New Testament canonizes
the Old, as Bishop Wordsworth said in his book
on The Canon.

Are you interested in religion for its own sake?
Does it satisfy you to know that Christianity is a
piece of supernatural information regarding the
way of salvation through Christ? Then take my
advice. Do not allow yourself to be disturbed by
Old Testament difficulties or diverted from what
for you is the central question of inquiry, What
think ye of Christ? If you settle that question
right, it is a matter of relatively minor importance
what you know about Jonah. Was Jonah crucified
for you or were you baptized in the name of
Jonah? I do not undervalue this and other questions, but I think that the settlement of them
should not be made a condition precedent to your
faith in Christ. The trouble is that there is a disposition on the part of some, apparently, to show
that unless the Bible is inerrantly accurate in everything you cannot trust it for anything. There are
those who seem to say that the order of a man's
thought must be first the inspired Bible and secondly the Divine Christ. To that position I cannot consent; and I am unable to make the *in ter-
rorem* argument that unless you believe in the inerrancy of the Bible you have no right to believe
in Christ. It is surely a strange apologetic which

says, 'Faith in Christ is all you need for salvation'; and then says 'You have no right to your faith in Christ unless you believe that the Bible is without error.' Moreover, a more fallacious argument could not be used than that which is sometimes employed in a misuse of the legal maxim, *Falsus in uno, falsus in omnibus.* How much history could stand this test? The real question is whether the Bible is true, not whether it is inspired. Must a book on every subject be inspired in order to be true? Have we lost all faith in inductive logic? Have we abandoned human testimony as a source of information? Is there no longer a place for the common sense of mankind?

Far more serious of course was the attack upon the New Testament, for in that the historicity of the Christian faith was involved, and we can well understand the feelings of the man who at one time might have said 'I wish I had the Four Gospels, for between the Epistles which I have and do not believe and the Gospels I would believe but do not possess, I am in a sorry plight.' But he need complain no more. The Gospels and the Epistles are both in his possession. The life of Christ and the story of the early Christian Church are in our hands. Is the record true? The fate of Christianity depends on the answer to this question. It is as if I were making a trip from New York to California and wished to know the best and shortest road. I satisfy myself by looking at a railway map and make my choice without hes itation; provided, however, that the map is accurately drawn. Satisfied on that score, at the proper hour I take my train. The Bible purports to tell you of the shortest, safest, and only road to Heaven. If you are satisfied that it tells the truth, take your train and have no fears.

(2) *Authority of the Bible*. It seems, therefore, that there is something to be said for each of the three claimants of which I spoke at the beginning of the lecture, and it is not difficult to see how their claims should be adjusted. A telegraph messenger, let us suppose, approaches a stranger and says 'A message for you, sir,' and the man replies 'I need no message, I have my reason.' 'Quite true,' says the messenger boy, 'you will need your reason to read the message, but this is the message.' The boy accosts another man. 'Cable for you, sir.' 'I need no cable, I have a radio outfit of my own.' 'That may be, sir,' says the messenger, 'but this did not come that way, and you would not have received it but for the cable. You need the cable to bring you the message, but this is the message.' So that the case stands thus: your reason to read the message, the Church to bring the message, but the Bible is the message. It is more than that, it is the only infallible rule of faith and practice. Thank the Church for bringing you the message, thank your reason for your ability to interpret the message, but the Bible is the message

which tells you "what we are to believe concerning God and what duties God requires of man." Thank God for it.

It is quite possible that some one who has done me the honor to read these lectures, may say, 'I believe the Bible to be the Word of God no matter what the critics say, and I wish that ministers would be satisfied to preach the Gospel and not trouble themselves with these fruitless speculations.' I confess that I could desire nothing better than that I might help you to arrive at this conclusion, but if you have arrived there without such help you are the more to be congratulated; for the important question is, whether you believe and not how you came to believe. If you are credibly informed that the train you wish to take goes at 10.30 A. M. and it does start at that time, you lose nothing because you failed to look at the time table— though I should not discourage that amount of precaution.

In the business of life men have no time to consider the reasons for all their beliefs. They draw freely upon the bank of common knowledge and make but few deposits. "The clerk in Eastcheap," as Carlyle said, "cannot be always verifying his ready reckoner." It is a pity, however, that men who read about the Bible do not take time to read the Bible itself. So many are like the man who, receiving a letter from a far off land, wastes time in looking at the postage stamp, deciphering the postmarks, identifying the handwriting on the envelope and wondering who has taken the trouble to write to him or what his motive was; when, if he would only open the letter all these questions would be answered in the reading. Why not open the letter at once, for "the cream of the correspondence," as Tony Lumpkin said, "is on the inside." The Bible is its own best witness and no amount of learning can supersede or make useless the feeling, born of intimacy with it, that it is the word of God.

It is easy, therefore, to understand the power which some men have in preaching. Some of those to whom I refer have no lack of learning, but they have also learned how to bring every thought into captivity unto the obedience of Christ. But some of them also lack learning. They read neither Greek nor Hebrew. They know little or nothing about the higher criticism. But they know the Bible. They know how to compare spiritual things with spiritual. They are on familiar terms with the great passages which feed their spiritual life. They are mighty in the Scriptures; and, in the witness which the Scriptures give to their own authority, these men have a full assurance of faith which scholarship alone will not give.

But something must be said on the other side. It is a great thing to know how the Bible has been vindicated, how attacks upon it have been answered, how assaults upon it have served to elicit new evidences in support of it which otherwise we may not have had. The bank that has passed triumphantly through a disastrous panic uses the fact as a valuable asset. You have great interests on land and sea, let us suppose, on which you wish to place large 'risks' and with a company of indisputable solvency. Here is one: 'Life, fire, marine and accident policies are written here.' Can you trust it? What do they say at the office? 'Scrutinize our history, look at our list of directors, read our last annual report—that will tell you about our assets and liabilities, surplus, volume of new business and the price of our stock in the market. Satisfy yourself on the basis of fact.' Is that not the position we are to take? Christianity is a great life insurance company, the greatest the world ever knew, with the largest possible promise of a life to come and a paid-up policy too, ready for everyone who is willing to trust it. Then I think we have no reason for sadness. The things that have happened to the Bible, as Paul said of his own troubles, "have fallen out rather to the furtherance of the gospel." But unbelief is spreading, you say. What of that? It need not take us by surprise; we were forewarned. "What if some do not believe? Shall their unbelief make the faith of God of none effect?"

a. Authority weakened. I must ask you now to consider two ways in which men, who themselves believe in the Scriptures, have at the same time been influenced by opinions which weaken the authority of the Scriptures. One of these is tradition; the other is the doctrine of the Christian consciousness. You cannot have two prices, so the political economists tell us, for the same commodity, in the same market, at the same time. The Roman Catholic Church holds a high theory of Biblical inspiration—*spiritu sancto dictante*, says the Council of Trent. But to a certain extent they have made the word of God of none effect through their tradition; not that tradition is without value, for an unbroken tradition as to the interpretation of a doctrine gives the doctrine an element of support. But when tradition is the only support of a doctrine, or is put in a place of competition with the teaching of the Bible, there is but one proper course to pursue and that is to disregard the tradition. On this subject Bishop Gore, in one of his recent books, speaks unequivocally in accordance with the formula used more than once in his writings: "The Church to teach, the Bible to prove."

The way in which the Christian consciousness weakens the authority of Scripture is still another form of the conflict between the letter and the spirit. Those who feel that they cannot be tied to the letter of the Scripture, seek to justify their independence of it on the ground that Christians under the guidance of the Holy Spirit are at liberty to put an interpretation on the Scripture which the lexical meaning of Scripture will not bear. The extreme position taken by Schleiermacher was of course a practical disavowal of the authority of the New Testament, and the doctrine of the Christian consciousness goes back to him, though his view regarding the authority of Scripture is not necessarily that of those at the present day who allow this doctrine to weaken it. According to Schleiermacher, the New Testament is the record of the Christian consciousness of the apostolic age; but the Christian consciousness of a later age may be different, and in so far as it may differ it has a right to supersede the record of the Christian consciousness of the early Church. The outcome of this principle would be that the Christian consciousness being in a state of constant flux, no one can predict what the consciousness of the next age will affirm, and therefore no one can put much confidence in what the Christian consciousness of the present age affirms.

But the New Testament is not what Schleiermacher said it was. It did bear testimony to the religious experience of the early Church, but that consciousness was an experience founded on the facts to which the New Testament bore testimony.

Experience may change, but facts remain the same. The facts being the same, the beliefs founded on the facts need not change, and the experience based on these beliefs will be the same. The same difficulties in religious faith which men feel now were felt then and were dealt with by the writers of the New Testament. The same blessed results of Christian faith which are felt to-day were felt in the early years of Christianity; and it is an argument in support of Christianity that men to-day have the same hopes, the same fears, the same doubts, the same joyful confidence that the first converts to Christianity experienced.

But let us look at this a little more closely. The Protestant doctrine of the Christian consciousness seems to occupy a position halfway between that of the Quaker's "inner light" and the Roman doctrine of infallibility, without the advantage of either. The Quaker, with his confidence in the inner light, may satisfy himself but does not pretend to make a rule for others, and if harm is done by his subjective states it is limited by the doctrine of individual illumination. The Roman Catholic justifies his departure from the teaching of Scripture on the ground that the Church being infallible has a right to speak in the present tense. These claims are met by a denial of the infallibility of the Church and stand or fall on that issue.

But what is the Christian consciousness? Is there any entity corresponding to this phrase? No; it is one of those hypostatized abstractions which, as we have seen, are made to carry so many burdens in philosophy. It really means an aggregate of individuals who entertain a certain belief. Is there any such thing as a *consensus* of belief among

Christian people which can be called the Christian consciousness? There is none, for to get it we should have to define a Christian as one who holds this conviction, and then we should reason in a circle. But if there is no *consensus* of opinion, there is no such thing as a Christian consciousness; and even if we had this *consensus* we should be where we were before, for each individual is fallible, and the question would be, How many fallibles does it take to make an infallibility? There is neither logic nor Scripture to support the doctrine of the Christian consciousness. But its effect on the interpretation of Scripture is not different from that of the infallibility of the Church. When the *Andover Review*, some years ago, undertook to modify the doctrine of eternal destiny in favour of a future state of probation, on the ground that the doctrine of the Christian consciousness was only the outcome of "putting the Lord's money out at usury," I took the liberty of asking whether this was not a step toward Rome. If on the principle referred to, it was right to say, 'Lord, thou gavest us the doctrine that except through faith one cannot be saved, and we have gained another doctrine beside it to the effect that except a man has had an opportunity to believe he cannot be lost,' does the Andover doctrine of "usury" differ much from the Roman which says, 'Lord, thou gavest unto us two sacraments, but we have gained five other sacraments besides them?' Is it more likely He would say to Andover than to Rome, "Well done good and faithful servant, enter thou into the joy of thy Lord?"

b. Authority reinforced. The arguments hitherto presented in behalf of the Bible are in the terms of probability. Outside of formal logic and mathematical reasoning there is no way of reaching certitude, that is to say, a state of mind in which the conclusions reached are not only justified but demonstrated. The question is whether there is any other process of thought by which certitude can be reached. No one has considered this question more seriously than John Henry, afterwards Cardinal Newman. He realized that outside of certain *a priori* convictions and deductive thought-relations it was impossible by the ordinary method of reasoning to go beyond probability. It was, therefore, possible to doubt the infallibility of the Church, for it was by a process of reasoning which could carry no further than probability that the inference respecting the infallibility of the Church was reached. What Newman desired was not only certitude but 'indefectible' certitude, a certitude, that is to say, which would insure against a possible change of opinion. This, the author thought, could be reached by what he called "the illative sense." What that illative sense is can hardly be stated in the few sentences which are at my disposal now, but should be learned from *The Grammar of*

Assent, in some respects the ablest book the author ever wrote.

In an article published many years ago[16] I tried to show that the attempt to secure certitude by the author's method, though made with an acumen for which Cardinal Newman was celebrated, and with a simple lucidity of style which has been rarely equalled, fell short after all of being successful. For suppose that one man by means of the 'illative sense' reached a position corresponding to 'indefectible certitude,' and another man by the same 'illative sense' reached a very different conclusion. How could these conflicting opinions justify certitude in either case? Each, it is conceivable, may have equal claims to indefectible certitude, but of what use is an indefectible certitude which points to two different results in this conflict of opinions? The existence of the opposite opinions reached by the same method would seem to show that the method had failed. For if the two opinions were contradictory, one or the other must be true; but which? And if not contradictory, both may be false. Cardinal Newman, it must be admitted, did not accomplish the task to which his rare gifts were devoted, and his attempt to find a logical stage coach which would take him from the railway station called 'Probability' to the door of his own soul, was a failure.

[16] "Newman's Grammar of Assent," *Princeton Review,* April, 1871.

Just as the Roman Catholic Church seeks certitude for the doctrine of the infallibility of the Church, so the Reformed theologians sought certitude for the infallibility of the Bible, the latter method being that which is known as the Witness of the Spirit—*testimonium spiritus sancti*—and it is affirmed that this is an argument that goes beyond probability by being the immediate testimony of the Spirit of God. Now, the idea that the individual is in such close relation to God as to give a sense of certitude is not confined to the theological doctrine here referred to; but something like it is found among Hegelian thinkers and the Mystics. There is no disposition on my part to dispute the truth of the doctrine. On the contrary, I believe that what the Hegelian and the Mystic believe is better taught and authoritatively taught in Holy Scripture. But if we stop to analyze the mental state here referred to, we shall find that the subject of this certitude is in a state of conviction, and that he infers that this subjective state is due to the witness of the Spirit. However probable it may be that the individual's subjective state which he calls certitude is produced in him by the Spirit of God, it remains possible that it was not; and the existence of this possibility reduces the certitude to the level of probability, a probability higher than that of ordinary testimony, because it is in addition to the probability afforded by ordinary testimony.

But, conceding to this subjective state all that

is claimed for it, either by Newman's *Grammar of Assent* or by the doctrine of the witness of the Spirit, it is a certitude from which the individual who has it derives benefit, but which he cannot make use of as a "common measure between minds" in arguing with another. *Nemo albus aliena albedine,* said the Remonstrant Curcellaeus in opposition to the doctrine of the imputation of Adam's sin; and similarly we may say, no man can be sure with another man's sureness. Of priceless value to the man who has it—for no man can be surer than sure—it is a personal possession which cannot be made over to another or used as an argument with one who has not had a similar experience. The man who has been convinced by argument may find the distance between probability and certitude covered by the witness of the Spirit, but for the man who has had no such experience the ordinary inductive proofs must suffice.

This doctrine, however, has been used, unwisely I think, to serve another purpose. For there are theologians who say that what we call apologetic theology can serve no good purpose, since those who have Christian faith do not need the apologetic, and those who lack this faith can derive no benefit from its defence. It is evident that a blind man cannot see a book even though it is under his nose, but it would be a rash conclusion to suppose that a man with normal vision can see it if it is not there. The blind man cannot read, but are we to conclude that all men are blind? Subjective difficulties may make a man proof against evidence, but are we to assume that no one would be impressed by evidence if it were placed before him? Have we a right to conclude that men with their eyes open see what has never been presented to them or do not need evidence to remove doubt or strengthen faith? Does it satisfy the requirements of duty to divide the world into two classes consisting of those who are blind and cannot read and those who can see and need not read? I confess that after a lifetime of belief in the Calvinistic theology as the most rational and the most scriptural of all systems of religious thought, I am not prepared to accept this extreme interpretation of it. Paul felt it was his duty to do his best to make all men see "what is the breadth and length and depth and height, and to know the love of Christ which passeth knowledge."

God's hidden purpose is no guide for our conduct. "The secret things belong unto the Lord our God: but those things which are revealed belong unto us and to our children." To see the truth and show it is our duty. There is no argument against a defence of Christianity which would not be equally good against preaching the Gospel. Moreover, the logical effect of the view of which I am speaking would be to take Christianity outside the sphere of inquiry altogether and give men an opportunity to say that the Gospel of Christ is as much a mystery religion as any other, indeed is something which only the initiated can understand and with which the uninitiated have no concern.

(3) *Inspiration of the Bible.* A threefold cord is not easily broken. In support of our Christian faith we have the indubitable testimony of history. That is to say we have the trustworthiness of the Bible. We have the conviction of its truth in our own subjective states produced in us, as we feel and the Scriptures assert, by the witness of the Spirit. In other words, we have the testimony of history confirmed by subjective inspiration. And in addition we have the objective inspiration of the Scriptures themselves. But just as the meaning of the witness of the Spirit needs careful interpretation, and the lack of it may be used to the disadvantage of Christianity, so the inspiration of the Scriptures may be affirmed in a degree that goes beyond the evidence of it and may be used in a way that is detrimental to the cause in behalf of which it is cited. Something therefore should be said in order that the use of this doctrine may be both sane and safe.

It is clear, to begin with, that the inspiration of the Scriptures is not a doctrine that supersedes the historical statements that support the truth of the Scriptures. For if the documents which teach this doctrine should prove to be untrustworthy or the passages in these documents which teach inspiration should turn out to be the interpolation of "a later hand," then the evidence for the inspiration of the Scriptures would be so weakened as to discredit the doctrine. And not only is this true, but it is also true that part of the evidence in support of the doctrine of Inspiration proceeds upon the assumption that certain other doctrines are true. We must have faith in Paul's right to speak when he says that he taught "not in words which man's wisdom teacheth but in words which the Holy Ghost teaches." We must believe in the Divine authority of Jesus before we can base an argument for the Inspiration of the Scriptures on the words "But the Scriptures cannot be broken." So that before we can logically reach the conclusion that the Scriptures are inspired, we must find in them sufficient evidence of their historic trustworthiness.

To this we are certainly brought, that we do not need the inspiration of the Scriptures to prove their inspiration. We cannot assume a doctrine in order to prove it. But if a doctrine so important as the inspiration of the Scriptures can be proved from Scripture without the presupposition of their inspiration, then other doctrines, such as the Divinity of Christ, can in like manner be proved without this presupposition. In fact, it is safe to say that we can on the simple historicity of the New Testament prove a fairly complete system of theology. The doctrine of the inspiration of the Scriptures is an induction based upon the teachings of the Scriptures. In other words, the facts and phe-

nomena of Scripture justify the belief that the
writers of the several books that compose the Bible
were under the controlling influence of the Holy
Ghost. This is the plain inference from what these
writers say. The inference, however, like other
inductions, is in the terms of probability. If
therefore the inspiration of the Scriptures is expressed in the terms of probability, we cannot logically claim a higher degree of conviction in regard
to what the Scriptures say. We cannot have the
authority of the Scriptures in the terms of probability and at the same time claim demonstration
for what the Scriptures say, for the stream cannot
rise higher than its source.

Conceding now the inspiration of Scripture, you
cannot on that account assume that it is errorless.
You may say that being inspired it is fair to expect
that it will be preserved from error, but this is not
evidence. We are accustomed in support of the
inspiration of the Bible to cite its accuracy; inspired, let us say, because errorless. It is a different
thing, however, to say errorless because inspired.
To say that the Bible is trustworthy because of its
accuracy is by implication to say that we have the
right and power to discern between truth and
error. You cannot license Reason to seek truth and
deny her right to see error. And it is a hazardous
thing to say that being inspired the Bible must be
free from error; for then the discovery of a single
error would destroy its inspiration. Nor have we

any right to substitute the word "inerrancy" for "inspiration" in our discussion of the Bible unless we are prepared to show from the teaching of the Bible that inspiration means inerrancy—and that, I think, would be a difficult thing to do.

This will serve to show how it is that some at the present day are saying that unless the Bible is without error it cannot be trusted for anything, and also how foolish such a statement is. Is there anything in all that is said about inspiration that can show us the exact area covered by inspiration and can tell us how far the mind of the Spirit and the mind of the author were coextensive in the writing of the Bible? Is there anything which assures us that Paul was as much under the influence of inspiration in sending for his cloak at Troas as in writing the Galatian Epistle? Then whatever you may think, however reasonable it is to suppose that the Spirit and Paul were concurrently active and in the same degree in all that Paul wrote, we cannot claim that this is explicitly stated or by fair inference logically deducible from anything said in the New Testament. With the deepest reverence for the Scriptures as the inspired word of God, I am nevertheless bound to say that differences of opinion on this point must be allowed to exist, as they have always existed, among Christians.

Let us suppose, however, that in the study of the Old Testament, for example, you felt compelled to modify certain preconceived opinions. Suppose that scientific proofs should compel you to put another interpretation upon the programme of creation, as it has compelled you to give another meaning to the word 'day,' would you give up the whole of the New Testament? Without pretending to any special scientific knowledge, it seems to me remarkable that the biblical account of creation which so wonderfully taught the essential truth of creation to man ages before science was born, still teaches it to scientific men if their prosaic science has not caused their imagination to suffer atrophy. But how foolish it would be to give up the Gospel simply because a dead literalism of interpretation would find no support in a modern text book on biology!

Probability is the guide of life, said Bishop Butler. The best ships afloat may be sunk at sea, but on that account do you take one known not to be seaworthy? You may prefer to stay ashore, but you cannot stay on this shore. The time is coming when you must embark. Will you refuse to take passage in the boat that carries Jesus because you still have some trouble about the one that carried Noah? It is a mistake to put the whole weight of the argument for Christianity on either the credibility of the Christian documents or their inspiration alone. I like to feel the force of the *a fortiori* argument. I like when I go to sea to know that the ship is provided with bulkheads and watertight

that you already regard as settled what you are seeking to prove?

If, however, men would only see that the great truths of Christianity do not depend upon the doctrine of inspiration, but stand in their own right and on the ground of the specific evidence which supports them, they would realize, perhaps, that without reasoning in a circle, these truths, though separately supported by specific arguments, have also in them an element of interdependence and support each other, just as we may say without any flaw of logic that the keystone of the arch keeps the stones on either side of it in their place and these stones at the same time keep the keystone from falling down. Here, for example, is a child's picture-puzzle, which the boy builds up, beginning in the centre or at one of the corners as he feels disposed, by finding, one after another, the piece in which the left-hand side fits the right-hand side of a piece already on the table; until, by and by, the picture is complete and the boy knows that he is right because each piece fits the other and all of them together make a complete picture.

Here also is the human body, with its circulatory, digestive, muscular and nervous systems, all related to one another, and each contributing to the well-being of the entire body. Or, to go further, let us remember that the body as a whole is made of microscopic cells each of which is a separate organism with power of growth, nourishment, and reproduction. The Scriptures long ago made us familiar with the idea that if one member suffer all the members suffer with it; but can we say that any one member is the cause of the well-being of any other member, in a sense which is not reciprocally true of that other member? Do these microscopic cells which make epithelial, muscular, or connective tissue, keep the larger organs like the liver, lungs and stomach, in a state of health? Or do these organs supply the conditions of life to the cellular system? Do these two sets of organs, the gross and cellular, stand to each other in the relation of cause and effect? and, if so, which is cause and which effect? Or are the two reciprocally cause and effect to each other? The latter of course is true; so that if the cellular life languishes the gross organs will not function properly, and if the gross organs are diseased the cellular life will suffer. In other words, these several systems in the body are organic to each other. I believe that something like this is true of the Bible in the relations which the Old and New Testaments sustain to each other.

It may be easier, as I have said, to proceed from the historical facts of the New Testament and the legitimate deductions which follow from them, to the story of the Old Testament. But one can hardly help seeing that the Bible is an organism and not a miscellaneous collection of writings. And the way to study it is to "see it steady and to see it whole," to realize it as a totality, the parts of which fit each other, supplement each other, support each other, and that through the whole the same "increasing purpose runs." *Mens agitat molem* is the conspicuous thing about the Bible. If we so regard it we shall see that a single idea rules the whole and that the Old Testament is a preparation for the New; that besides the temporal interests of Israel and, indeed, as part of them, there was an outlook as to Israel's place in the preparation of the world for Christ. With all this in our minds there will be no difficulty in accepting, without putting a hard and fast interpretation upon it, the doctrine of the inspiration of the Scriptures. We shall accept without cavil the texts which specially teach it. Without forcing a meaning upon them in the interests of one theory, or denying what they say in the interests of another theory, without being disturbed over "various readings" or the subtleties of exegesis, we can accept these texts as confirming what an impartial study of the Bible would lead us to expect; so that while we believe that in "the olden time" holy men of God spoke as they were moved by the Holy Ghost, we can also believe that we have a more sure word of prophecy whereunto we do well to take heed.

But the naturalistic critic is determined to see nothing but the operation of natural causes in all that bespeaks purpose, and that paves the way for the Christian dispensation. Having, therefore, an antecedent conviction adverse to inspiration he picks holes in all the texts which affirm it, tells us that we reason in a circle, that the suppressed premise in our enthymeme is unproved, and that we reach the height of our argument by piling question-begging inferences upon each other until we have built a pyramid which from top to bottom is a fallacious sorites.

But so many men on both sides of this great controversy, which carries with it every interest that makes life worth living, lack imagination and the seer's gift. They are the "wooden vessels" in the great house of learning and might easily be dispensed with. The spirit of the Old Testament has not touched them enough to make them see that it breathes in purpose. They are so anxious to show that it is not divine that they do not stop to see that it is human. They do not appreciate the fact that the Bible is a bow of promise as well as a book of duty; that with matchless art it can pack a page of precept in a line of epigram; that its stories suggest homely duties as well as open chapters in the movement of Providence; that good men are painted without excessive praise and bad men are spoken of in the blunt ruggedness of fact, and not in the half concealng, half revealing way of modern art which makes vice enticing. They do not see that topics for the times on which the prophet speaks are also lessons for all time. They read with a prosaic literalism his message to the men of his day, but do not see the far-off look on his face which carries his meaning down the ages. No wonder, then, that the Old Testament is sundered from the New. No wonder that under the doctrine of naturalistic uniformitarianism, the New Testament, bereft of miracle and no longer heir of prophecy, is found to be but a shrivelled remnant of the Jewish faith. No wonder that this outcropping of Jewish modernism, speaking in terms of a lofty thought and an emotional philosophy of love, feels no need of a Divine Saviour, repudiates the expiation of sin, and putting the cross of individual self-sacrifice in place of the one to which was nailed the suffering Saviour of the world, parades "salvation by character" as the be-all and end-all of the new Christianity.

"Choose ye this day whom ye will serve. If Baal be God serve him, if the Lord be God serve Him." We come ultimately to the old issue of choice between contradictory alternatives. Let us not multiply issues. Him that is weak in the faith receive ye, but not to doubtful disputations. Let none be made an offender for a word. Let us not drive the ploughshare of division between the friends of Christ. But, ultimately, we are logically forced to choose between a naturalistic and a supernaturalistic explanation of the Bible. And if we wish to keep the Christianity which teaches salvation by faith in Jesus Christ, we are shut up to a doctrine of the inspiration of the Bible. Taking it in respect to the relations of the Old and

New Testaments to each other, taking it as a whole whose parts are organic to each other and the whole, there is no way of denying its inspiration which does not put its leading doctrines in jeopardy. Let us look then at the Bible as an organic whole; follow the trend of the Old Testament teaching along the level path of history, into the byways of precept, story and epigram, up the slopes of prophetic vision, and on to the mountain tops of religious aspiration. For this is the Bible's way. It speaks in didactic narrative, persuades by fervid argument, soars in lofty verse, and sings in a melody that stirs the deepest feelings of our being. All that the prophets foretold is fulfilled in the New Testament, all the hopes they fostered are realized in it. The Incarnation crowns the great story of Divine fellowship with men; and the New Testament message is a commission and command to preach the gospel of salvation to a perishing world.

The Bible presents to us a panorama of the Divine purpose. As we look we see the unfolding of the great drama of sin and salvation. As we listen to its majestic music from the creation overture in Genesis to the hallelujah chorus in the Apocalypse, we realize that we have been holding in our hands the inspired *libretto* of God's great oratorio of Redemption.

violent attack, but usually has a long period of incubation. The minister who is the subject of it has doubts which he carries in his soul a long time before he speaks of them. But by cautious reticence in regard to the dubious and convincing fervour respecting the obvious, this mental state need cause him no serious inconvenience. Yet let us not be uncharitable. Theology is a country that exposes a large frontier to attack, and we may well sympathize with him who resembles another of whom it was said:

> He fought his doubts and gathered strength,
> He would not make his judgment blind,
> He faced the spectres of the mind
> And laid them; thus he came at length
> To find a stronger faith his own.

But nevertheless the fact remains that a man of this class is like him who said to Jesus, "Lord, I believe: help thou mine unbelief." He believes to-day, and disbelieves to-morrow. His is an intermittent faith. His convictions are strong to-day and weak to-morrow. He has a fluctuating faith. The relations of faith and unbelief in his case are like those of pleasure and pain in the common experience of mankind: you cannot tell whether they follow each other in rapid succession, whether they mingle and form a *tertium quid* called doubt, or whether they preserve a simultaneous separateness in the flow of thought.

As in other matters connected with disease, we

naturally inquire into the etiology of this New Christianity. Some suppose that it is due to a better knowledge of the New Testament Greek, resulting in a better understanding of its meaning; to a better appreciation of the historical conditions under which the books of the Old and New Testaments came into existence; or to a more subtle psychological insight into the spirit of Christianity. But this at best is only a very partial explanation of the facts with which we are dealing; for many of the differences of belief which are now so conspicuous, existed long before the new learning came into being. The New Christianity is due to a new attitude. This new attitude toward the Bible produces a new attitude toward Christianity, just as a new attitude toward Christianity results in a new attitude toward the Bible. But the deeper reason for the spread of the epidemic of which I am speaking is to be found in a new attitude toward the universe which inevitably results in a new attitude toward both the Bible and Christianity.

Philosophy and science have led men to take a uniformitarian view of the world. This may show itself in a spiritual or a materialistic way. Whether you consider the world as mind and the world-process as the gradual unfolding of a system of thought-relations, or whether you regard it as matter and the world-process as the gradual change from simple to complex relations, in either case the process is a gradual one, proceeding without

that Christianity is a piece of supernatural information in respect to the salvation of mankind. That this is what it claims to be there can be no manner of doubt, whatever the evidence be that supports it. If men are in no peril, there is no need of salvation. If there is no adequate provision for salvation in Christianity, then Christianity is useless.

It will be generally agreed that the authoritative information in regard to salvation is contained in the Bible, and it is also the general belief of Christians that the Bible is not only the record of supernatural information, but also that it is a supernatural record. The two ideas are obviously distinct. Let us then consider it as a record of supernatural information. Men differ, however, in the interpretation of this record. The existence of the various Christian denominations is evidence of this, for these denominations exist largely for the sake of promulgating doctrines which represent these differences. There are, that is to say, what are called "witness bearing churches." Yet in spite of these differences, there is a core of doctrine which is commonly regarded as containing the essence of the Christian faith. Clearly, then, there is an area of difference among Christian people which does not menace the right of those who stand for these differences to bear the name of Christians. And though the Scriptures which contain the record of supernatural revelation were not themselves supernaturally given, we should not on that account deny the divine authority of the Christian religion. It would be very foolish and very unreasonable to do so.

Still, believing as the Christian world always has believed and still believes that these Scriptures were given by inspiration of God, there are and always have been differences of opinion as to the nature of inspiration, the area covered by it, and the sense in which the Scriptures are infallible. You cannot call in question a man's Christian faith because he has not studied and so does not understand the problem involved in the inspiration of the Scriptures; or, having studied, has come to a conclusion differing from our own.

The doctrine of inspiration is based on an inductive study of the contents of Scripture, and, like all other inductions, is expressed in the terms of probability and may undergo modification if the facts of Scripture can be shown to be misinterpreted. We must believe this or else take the Scriptures out of the sphere of inquiry altogether, in which case the argument for the inspiration of the Scriptures would rest upon the subjective certitude of the individual, and that cannot be a basis of argument between men who differ. For men possessed of this certitude, then, Christianity would rest upon supernatural information, supernaturally recorded, and in the mind of the individual believer supernaturally accredited. This in fact is

conditions but not the other, and I venture to say that nearly all of the New Christianity of which I am speaking can be accounted for by considering these two classes of men.

iii

FACE VALUE BUT NOT TOTALITY

Let us then consider those who take the Scriptures at their face value but not in their totality. Men of this class limit their attention to the Gospels, particularly to the three synoptic Gospels. Christianity, they say, is the religion of Jesus, and Jesus was a man—only a man. They err, of course, in taking this view of what these Gospels teach, but they take them in good faith for what they believe to be their teaching. And so believing, they accept Jesus as their religious authority and guide. But why? Because, they say, he is the founder of our religion; he is our teacher and example; and moreover he is to us the revealer of God. Let us examine these reasons.

a.   Jesus is the Founder of Christianity, and being the founder of a great religion is worthy of great respect, and the greater the religion the greater is the respect due to his memory. But does the greatness of the religion make the founder great, or does the greatness of the founder give greatness to the religion? Does it make so much difference who was the founder of the order of Rotarians? Would these clubs which are proving themselves so beneficent throughout the world be of less value if you did not know the founder's name? Put all the honour you please upon the name of Jesus; if he is only human the most you can make of Christianity is that a human being founded a human society.

> Now he is dead! far hence he lies
> In the lorn Syrian town;
> And on his grave, with shining eyes,
> The Syrian stars look down.

Make what you can of Christianity on the supposition that Jesus was simply a human being: "You can only hang a painted object on a painted nail," as Whewell of Cambridge said many years ago.

b. But, you say, 'He is our authority because he was a great teacher': "Never man spake like this man." Yet other men have been great teachers; Epictetus was, so was Seneca, and so was Marcus Aurelius. But Jesus according to your view was only a man, and dead, as they are.

Again, do you honour Jesus because you accept his teaching, or do you accept his teaching because he spoke with authority? If the former, then having been put in possession of the teaching you no longer need the teacher. You learned your elementary mathematics from a schoolmaster, but having learned them you no longer need the schoolmaster. You recognize Gray's "Elegy in a Country Churchyard" as a beautiful poem, but had it been

Green's, or White's, or Black's elegy, it would have been none the less beautiful. Again, can you say that the ethics of Jesus, wonderful as they are, may not have been arrived at by another human being? We have had other ethical teachers. Students of philosophy are familiar with the maxim of Socrates that no one does wrong wilfully and therefore that virtue is a matter of knowledge; with Aristotle's advice about avoiding extremes; and with the Stoics' "wise man." Can we say that it was impossible that another thinker than Jesus might have built his ethics on the doctrine of love?

The ethics of Jesus do not prove that he was more than human, I concede; and being as you suppose only human, you cannot say that his teaching is not open to revision. The pupil is rarely a 'carbon copy' of the master. The history of Greek philosophy shows a succession of teachers, each of whom tries by revision, amendment, or by sharp antithesis, to improve on the teaching of his predecessor, and this went on until at the end the teaching of the Academy became a weak syncretism of previous masters. If Jesus was only human, can you find fault with those who at this moment are endeavoring to revise his ethics on the plea that what suited the simple life of Galilean fishermen is not adapted to the complicated civilization in which we are living? It is open to you undoubtedly to take the position of Nicodemus and say that Jesus was "a teacher come from God," but with your postulate of a non-miraculous religion you will not have the same good reason that Nicodemus had for believing that he came from God.

But do not misunderstand me, I am not minimizing the value of Jesus' teaching. You cannot say too much in its praise to suit me. But I maintain that if he were simply a human being his ethics need not and could not be exempt from criticism. The truth, however, is that ethical teaching was not the central fact in the ministry of Jesus. He did not come to open a school but to train a body of men whom he was to send out into the world to preach the gospel of the Kingdom; but above everything else, he came to die, the just for the unjust, that he might bring us to God.

yes this is true

c. Again, you say, he is our authority, for he not only taught us but lived the life which he preached. That is true, and it is an argument in favour of his divinity, but we are now thinking of those who regard him as only a man. Let us, however, look at this phase of his life. He "left us an example that we should follow in his steps," the great outstanding feature so far as his example is concerned being in his vicarious death, a matter which will occupy our thought in another lecture. But looking at him simply as a human being, his example is particularly manifested in his friendships. What a lesson he gave us! What a wonderful thing friendship is! To what base uses men put it! So often do they treat it as a ladder on which they may rise to place and power, and then throw it down. Men drop their friends; without reason, unless it be that their power for service is exhausted. But the world is not without examples of loyal, devoted, self-sacrificing friendship. We have the story of Damon and Pythias in heathen legend and of Saul and Jonathan in sacred history. We have wonderful illustrations of friendship too among young men, and the group of which Jesus was the centre was composed mainly of young men. Read Milton's "Lycidas" and see how he loved his college friend. Read in Arnold's "Thyrsis" the story of his love for the poet Clough. Take down your "In Memoriam" once more and see how Tennyson loved Arthur Hallam. See there how art, science, philosophy and religion placed wreaths on Hallam's bier; and how the chambers of the poet's soul were stripped of their richest furnishings to give a solemn grandeur to the poet's grief. In this matter of friendship Jesus is an outstanding example; but does that entitle him to our worship? Does he not in the very evidence of his friendship show that he is more than man? Let us see.

The word "friend" is the most reciprocative word in the vocabulary of human love. Ties of blood do not always reveal this reciprocity of feeling, but where friendship exists each is a friend to the other. And yet there is a certain delicacy of sentiment which makes it easier for one to say 'He is my friend' than to say 'I am his friend.' And this difference is indicated in the way Jesus speaks of his disciples. "Ye are my friends," he said. But he said it in the full consciousness of the distance that lay between himself and them. Royalty may condescend, but it seldom abdicates. Would any one of the friends to whom I have referred have said to the others: "Henceforth I call you not servants, but I have called you friends?" We cannot understand this language between these friends except upon the assumption that it was the Lord of Glory who, being also man, condescended to call these humble disciples his friends. It is this subtle union of Godhead with manhood which gives point to the fellowship of Jesus with his disciples and explains the union of a remote dignity with a familiar condescenion. And were it not that we read this unique relation of Jesus and the twelve into the story, it would cease to have any special value for us, being only the story of an exceptional friendship which for long ages has ceased to exist.

d. But it is said by those whom we have in view, 'Jesus is our authority because he has revealed God.' Let us consider that. Does it mean that he revealed to us the fact that God exists? Remember that the class of men to whom I refer have, for the most part, abandoned the old arguments for the existence of God which are found in the world of things, and profess now to find a sufficient argument in the earthly life of Jesus. Do

unfolding of a set of categories. Thesis, antithesis, and synthesis are the magic words with which the Hegelians explain the universe. I affirm, you deny; but a third man says, 'You are both wrong, but your differences can be reconciled in a higher unity.' Black and not-black are contradictories; but brown is a higher unity in which this difference is reconciled. This is not exactly Hegelian, but it is very much like some of the Hegelian methods of reconciling contradictions. The philosophy to which I refer is a very logical system and a coherent one, but Christianity is an historical religion and rests on a foundation of fact.

You cannot make facts out of syllogisms any more than you can sell lots in Utopia. The spider's web is a very beautiful structure and we admire it as we see it shining in the sunlight. But woe to the unwary fly that is enmeshed in it. It is small comfort to him to know that this wonderful piece of architecture was spun out of the maker's own substance. Small comfort is it to us to know that this Hegelian system is the product of a brain which Lord Haldane calls the greatest since Aristotle, if the logical result is to destroy Christianity. And this is what it does, when you consider the effect it has upon our conception of Christ and the nature of his work. For the outcome of its teaching (at least according to some Hegelians) is that Christ is a mythical representation of the presence of God in the soul of man. Every man therefore in a certain sense is an incarnation. And when you get this idea you do not need the historical exhibition of it, any more than the man who is looking for the active principle of a plant and has extracted from it the codeine and mophia, wishes to be burdened with the vegetable tissue from which he obtained it. What need have we of the flaming poppy fields of history once we get from them the "dull narcotic" that deadens pain and fills us with a fictitious peace?

Turning then to the work of Christ, see the transvaluation of values—to use Nietzche's phrase —which follows this view of Christianity. For all the Gospel is summed up, say the men of this school, in the words "Die to live." The law of life is self-sacrifice. The dramatic exhibition of the duty was seen in the death of Christ; but the performance of it is left to the soldier. Jesus is the symbol, the soldier the reality. Nothing can save us from this lame and impotent conclusion if we deny the Scriptural doctrine of Christ's vicarious sacrifice. Driven to this decision, the death of Christ from the side of the chief priests was a wanton murder, and from the side of Christ himself a needless martyrdom. Is it possible for us to put this Hegelian construction on the person and work of Christ? Let us see. Was Jesus an Hegelian? Did he plan or connive at this theatrical performance only to impress us with the idea that our sufferings may be a benefit to others, and that it is up the rough stairway of pain that we ourselves attain a higher and better manhood? No, it would be blasphemous to read this meaning into the sacred narrative.

Was Paul an Hegelian? Did he renounce his ancestral faith and spend his remaining days in the hardships of a missionary life, preaching forgiveness of sins and making appeals to the hopes and fears of men by the doctrine of a future life, knowing all the time that the real thing to be accomplished was an improvement in the manners of those to whom he preached? Then Christianity is an imposture and, if it was based upon a falsehood, deserves to be scathingly exposed; and the honeyed words in which the Hegelian writers describe it are only a flattering condescension to the feelings of those innocent people who take their religion seriously and as meaning what it says.

Or again, was Paul an unconscious Hegelian? Did he act in good faith when he was determined to know nothing among men but Jesus Christ and him crucified; when, coveting no man's silver or gold, seeking as he said "not yours but you," he preached among the Gentiles what he called "the unsearchable riches of Christ"? In dead earnest himself, has it been left to us to discover that the purpose of God was not what Paul thought it was, but rather that by appeals to the religious nature of man the cause of morality might be promoted, and that by the alluring hope of heaven and the lurid dread of hell the great cause of peace on earth and good will to men might be advanced? If this were so, then we have evidence which had never occurred to us before, that Paul was under the inspiration of the Spirit in that he went on preaching until his death "not knowing what the Spirit of Christ that was in him did signify when he testified concerning the sufferings of Christ and the glory that should follow."

Are we to believe that there has been beneath the letter of the New Testament and hidden from the "babes" who put their trust in it, gave their lives in defence of it, and won the victories of faith which have shaped the fortunes of the civilized world, a cryptic meaning of the gospel revealed only in these later days to the "wise and prudent" philosophers of the Hegelian school? No. Men may not accept the miraculous facts of Christianity, they may be materialtists or agnostics, but with the Bible in their hands they will not risk their reputation enough to say that this is the meaning of Christianity. This being the case, can we, with the utmost appreciation of the fine feeling which writers of this school so abundantly evidence and of the reverent tone in which they speak of Jesus, say that the Hegelian interpretation of Christianity is Christianity? Surely this is impossible. And that I may describe this philosophical interpretation of our holy religion with proper respect for the profound thought and religious feeling which pervades it, and with full recognition of its merits and defects, I crave the privilege of calling it a *philosophate* of Christianity.

2. The Naturalistic Interpretation of Christianity. According to this view the history of human experience is interpreted in the terms of matter, and the origin of Christianity will resolve itself into the simple statement that Jesus attempted to effect a revolution and failed; unless we adopt the Darwinian interpretation of morality and say that it is only one of Nature's tricks whereby she seeks to secure 'the healthful perpetuity of social tissue.'

This unwarrantable intrusion of purposive activity into a materialistic theory of the universe whereby a metaphor is made to serve the purpose of reality, only shows how hard it is to escape from the persistent demands of our rational nature and in itself is an argument against the naturalistic theory of conduct. But on the supposition that the Darwinian interpretation of conduct is a true account of the genesis of moral ideas, we must believe that in order to secure her end, it was necessary for Nature to find means to induce men to live peaceably together; and that therefore she has lured us with hopes and lashed us with fears, that she has invented a spurious doctrine of immortality, and has found her most effective agency in a great constabulary of priests, presbyterian ministers, and the like, who by preaching the doctrine of rewards and punishments in a future life are helping men to live harmoniously in the life that now is. This is truthful testimony, however, to the value of the Christian ministry; and when we are told that the clergyman's average stipend is less than a policeman's pay, we can well afford to say to our brethren in the ministry in all Christian denominations: be of good cheer, ye are of more value than many policemen.

Conceding, however, that there may be truth in this conception for which the naturalistic thinkers have contended, what are we to think of those philosophers who are trying to undo Nature's work? Educated by illusion into a belief in right and wrong, what will happen when the world has been disillusioned by the adoption of a Darwinian ethic; and to what agency shall we turn in order that men may cease to do evil and learn to do well? What shall we do when we part with the 'survival value' of belief in a future state? Adopting a naturalistic theory of conduct, the most we could do would be to trust that "if hopes were dupes, fears may be liars." But are they? *Tantum religio potuit suadere malorum?* says Lucretius. What a lot of trouble religion has cost us. But has religion occasioned the fears, or have fears given rise to religion? Does naturalism solve our questions? Does it disclose the great secret of death? The young man who attends regularly at boat-drill on the steamer, under the impression that it is intended

up the Kingdom of God on the earth. That being the case, we may expect to hear some good preaching and shall not be disappointed. The pulpit will speak loudly against crime and fraud and drunkenness. It will use great plainness of speech regarding the corrupting influence of contemporary pleasures, though men and women will continue to read the books which reveal skilled performance on the tight rope of erotic feeling, and hazardous conversation on the psychology of sex. It will flame with indignation against war, while all the time the pews will hold the greatest menace to peace in the men who clamour for their share in the oilfields of the backward nations. It will continue to advocate large collections for colleges and missions and will have great success until the faith which inspired the benevolence has spent its force. And when the Martha type of religion grows tired, there will come into prominence the Mary type which craves the quiet hour and seeks shelter from the midday heat within the church's open door where it can spend an hour in humble, grateful prayer.

But all the while men will be losing faith in personal immortality and those who have given themselves up to the New Christianity will have but little to say to the man who feels that life's fitful fever is nearly over and asks, 'Whither am I going?' Then perhaps we shall find that we are not doing our full duty when in our public worship we pray to a value-judgment God, sing a value-judgment hymn, listen to a value-judgment sermon, partake of a value-judgment communion, baptize our children in the name of a value-judgment Trinity, and bury our beloved dead in the sure and certain hope of a value-judgment immortality.

Let us then consider the 'value-judgment,' for it is the key to the Ritschlian interpretation of Christianity. You enjoy music, let us say, and whether it be the "Dead March in Saul," the "Ninth Symphony," or the "Wedding March in Lohengrin" to which you have been listening, you are really receiving pleasure in a series of mental states which terminate when the music stops. You express your appreciation in appropriate words, and this expression is a value-judgment meaning that it was worth something to you to have had this experience of pleasure. A man after business hours sits in his library and, over his cigar, thinks of the money he expects to make and how when he gets it, he will use it. He will portion his children, patronize Art, contribute to great benevolent schemes, enjoy travel, and indulge himself in luxurious surroundings. 'That will be fine,' he says, as he gives expression to a value-judgment. The objective possession of a fortune is not necessary to his enjoying the pleasure of disposing hypothetically of one which as yet exists only in his imagination. You have your mother's picture, and

But you may none the less enjoy religious services. A man without any religious convictions may be impressed by the 'solemn ritual of the dead,' and a stately service may have a subduing and elevating effect upon the frivolous. Your religion as the result of this conception of it stands in the same category with other values, and you feel that neither they nor it stands in need of any objective reality. Whether therefore you go to church or go to the opera, it is a fine thing sometimes to get away from the grinding world of fact, of production and distribution, of debits and credits, of trade and politics, of selfishness and greed, and live for a little while in the better world of values.

But then what happens? Religion becomes a form of pleasure. Symbolism instead of being an aid to faith becomes an object of faith. Instead of the beauty of holiness we shall begin to talk of the holiness of beauty, and, as Höffding says, religion will be regarded as a device for the conservation of values. Instead of art and poetry lifting us up to high levels of religious thought, we shall let our religion down to the lower level of art and poetry. Save as a form of pleasurable emotion religion will be dead, and our solemn rites and stately rituals, like costly flowers on the coffin of a corpse, will serve only to hide the melancholy truth from our eyes. So that instead of regarding God as the basis of religion and the 'home of values,' the institutions of religion are reduced to the ineffectual function of keeping in active operation the common moralities of life. The greater is made servant to the less and a discredited religion, though it speaks in the name of God, is reduced to the place of keeping alive in the breasts of men an appreciative estimate of the True, Beautiful, and Good. The truth of the whole matter is that many men are living to-day in a fool's paradise of subjectivity. Religion is a feeling; God is a state of mind. But the end of this is not hard to discern, and in the case of a great many, I fear, religion will share the fate of the German mark which had subjective value so long as it represented objective reality, but when it came to have only subjective value lost even that.

There are several kinds of scepticism. There is an intellectual scepticism which, beginning with an attempt to know too much, ends in knowing nothing. There is also an emotional scepticism which, discarding all attempts to have a reasoned faith, is satisfied with what is sometimes called the theology of the feelings. There are Christians of this type, and it is descriptive, I have no doubt, of a great many who call themselves Ritschlians. Making no attempt to solve difficult problems of religious belief they content themselves with a simple trust in Christ, 'believing where they cannot prove.' There are others who, with an undefined accept-

one of the intermediate stations. The danger, however, is that you may get into the wrong train, and that it may be only when the "limited" is pulling out of the station and you feel the rumble of the wheels under your feet that the conductor will put his head inside the door of your parlour car and say: "This train makes no stops; the next station is agnosticism."

CHAPTER IV
THE PERSON OF CHRIST

THE primitive Christian community regarded Jesus as both God and man. Of this there can be no doubt. But it was a totality of impression that constituted their mental state, just as in a single undiffereniated act of consciousness we recognize a rose without stopping to distinguish between the petals, stamens, and pistils which constitute it. But this synoptic apprehension of the divine-human Jesus could not last, or rather men could not long be satisfied with it. Difficulties of an intellectual kind would suggest themselves. Differences of opinion would arise, and it would be necessary to define and defend the truth represented by this totality of impression.

i

CHALCEDONIAN CHRISTOLOGY

This necessity arose, as has been already implied, in many ways. There were those who simply sought a fuller explication of the doctrine of the two natures; and then there were those who denied one or the other of the two elements which entered into this primitive conception, the result being that

mode in which the human and the divine were united in Jesus, and great differences of opinion developed themselves. There were the Docetae who said that Christ was not a man and that his human body was only an appearance and not a reality. There were the Apollinarians who admitted that he had a real human body but affirmed that he had no human soul, since in him the divine nature took the place of the human soul; that is to say, they admitted that Jesus had the *psyche* common to all living things, but not the *pneuma* or rational soul. The debate ended by affirming that Christ had a "true"—that is a real body, and "a reasonable soul"—forms of expression adopted at the Council of Chalcedon and embodied in the creeds of Christendom ever since.

Then came the question how these two elements in the Person of Christ were related to each other. He was God and he was man. Then he must have had a divine nature and a human nature. But this started another debate, for the Eutychians said, 'No; not two natures, but one, the two natures blending and forming a *tertium quid*'; very much, I suppose, as an acid and an alkali unite to form a neutral salt. But the Eutychian doctrine was condemned, and it was affirmed that Christ had two whole, entire, and distinct natures which existed side by side without mixture or confusion. There was still room, however, for difference of opinion; for the Nestorians said that if he had two natures there must be two persons in Christ, a human and a divine. But this position was negatived also, and the full doctrine of the Person of Christ was formulated at the Council of Chalcedon in 451 A.D. and has been from that day to this the accepted doctrine of the Christian Church.

It may seem strange that the intellectual interest of the Church during the first four centuries of our era turned on questions regarding God, the Trinity, and the Person of Christ. The problem of sin with the correlative doctrine of salvation came later, under the influence of Augustine, and still later at the time of the Reformation when the great question of Soteriology underwent discussion. Whether it was the influence of Hellenizing thought, or whether it was a true instinct which led the Church to begin at the beginning, may not be easy to decide; but it is clear that all the later problems depend for solution upon the meaning and implications of the doctrine of the Person of Christ, and therefore it is well that the first effort of the Church was to give an explicit answer to the question, What think ye of Christ?

Later questions in regard to the Chalcedonian Christology have been raised which do not seriously affect or modify it; but they have occupied little place in controversy, and being only the speculations of theologians have not affected the life of the Church in any very appreciable degree. There is, for example, the view which is called the doctrine of *Kenosis,* according to which it is said that Christ by a voluntary act of self-depotentiation made it part of his work of humiliation while on earth not to know some things. There are different forms of this doctrine which grows out of the passage in Philippians ii.7, where it is said "he made himself of no reputation," literally "emptied himself," (ἑαυτὸν ἐκένωσεν); and also out of an attempt to explain the passage in Mark xiii.32, which says "Of that day and that hour knoweth no man, not even the Son, but the Father." This view has had considerable advocacy by theologians in America and Great Britain, and Bishop Gore is perhaps the ablest representative of it now in the English-speaking world.

The doctrine of an impersonal human nature in Christ has also given trouble to some theologians, it being difficult to see how the Divine person can "act," as some express it, the human nature. We may think of crude material analogies, as for instance, when hot water and cold are drawn from the same tap; but they do not solve the problem. There are, however, those who think that the identification of Jesus with mankind loses some of its meaning when the human nature of Jesus is supposed to operate only through his Divine Person. I do not care to be wise above what is written, nor do I think that the question which is raised can be answered. Least of all do I feel that it is solved by Dr. Sanday who invokes the aid of the "subliminal consciousness" in the interpretation of this mystery.[1] I confess that such speculations do not interest me because they can throw no light on what is obviously an insoluble problem, and it seems to me that Dr. Sanday was too ready to take advantage of the results of speculative psychology.

If, however, the Chalcedonian doctrine of an impersonal human nature in the constitution of the Person of Christ were to undergo amendment, it would run counter to the doctrinal authority of a general council—as that at Chalcedon is admitted to be. Whatever then may be the opinion of individual theologians, no amendment to the teachings of Chalcedon could be allowed by the Roman Catholic Church or the Catholic party of the Anglican Church. Holding, however, as I do, to a Confession of Faith which affirms that general councils may err and have erred, I have no difficulty in saying that no general council has a right to put barriers in the way of a search for truth. The controversy which occupied the attention of men during the greater part of the nineteenth century was really a debate on the merits of the Chalcedonian Christology, and to some of the questions raised by that debate we must now give our attention.

---

[1] Sanday, *Christology and Personality*.

ii

THE CHALCEDONIAN CHRISTOLOGY ATTACKED

1. Under the influence of Strauss it was held that the Gospels were not written until some time late in the second century and that during this period belief in the man Jesus had by myth or legend been transformed into belief in a supernatural incarnation; in other words, that the man Jesus had undergone a process of deification. This led to a discussion of the origin of the Gospels and the vindication of their early origin completely disposed of the mythical or legendary hypothesis. Mark was held to be the earliest gospel with an Urmarkus as antecedent to the Gospel as we now have it—Matthew and Luke containing common materials which are supposed to come from prior documents, one of which recorded the sayings of Jesus (logia) and the other the narrative portions. About this, differences of opinion exist among critical students, and however their differences may be settled it is undoubtedly true that the substantial portions of Gospel history go back to a time not later than from twenty to thirty years after the Crucifixion. This was a death blow to the mythical theory which regarded Jesus as a deified man. The outcome of the same critical investigation of the origin of the other books of the New Testament gave us the great epistles by Paul, *i.e.* the Romans, Galatians, and Corinthians as the indubitable work of

their reputed author. The attempt, therefore, to destroy Christian faith by a short, sharp, and decisive attack upon the capital of Christianity signally failed. Whatever may happen, it is decisively settled that between the death of Christ and the publication of the synoptic Gospels there was no time for the development of a myth, that is to say, for a process of deification whereby the man Jesus came to be regarded by the primitive Christian community as a Divine being. That ended, criticism busied itself with the dissection of the Gospels themselves, and to this I will return later.

But the mythical theory though defeated was not destroyed, for a similar attempt in recent years has been made in a different direction. No longer encamped in front of Calvary, the forces of the enemy went behind the Cross and there entrenched themselves. Their problem is not to show that the human Jesus was deified in the minds of his followers; but that the early Christians were worshipping a humanized God and that Christianity really had its origin in a vegetable or solar myth: in other words, that Christianity is nothing more than a phase of Paganism in which under various names the sun-god, or the principle of vegetative life, was worshipped. According to this view Christianity is just a study in comparative religion. If this hypothesis of its origin were true Jesus would take his place in the pantheon of heathen gods. Jesus

Jesus is as absurd as to doubt the existence of Alexander the Great.

Notice now the logical effect of this latest mythical theory. Said the mythologists of the school of Strauss: 'The primitive Christians worshipped a deified man'; say the mythologists of the school of Drews: 'The primitive Christians worshipped a humanized God.' Who is to judge between these two schools? Will you say that the early Christians worshipped a man who was afterwards regarded as God? Or will you stand with those who say that they worshipped a heathen God under the name of a man who never existed? Or will it not be more reasonable to say that they worshipped a being whom they regarded as both God and man? Putting the two mythological interpretations together they make a strong argument for the Chalcedonian Christology; and assuming that there is a basis of truth in both views, the conflicting position of the mythologists suggests that Jesus was neither a humanized God nor a divinized man, but that the faith of the primitive Christians was that he was both God and man.

2. But let us understand what the motive of these criticis is. Antisupernaturalism is their postulate. At all costs they must be rid of the doctrine of the Incarnation; and still they have something to say. There is Schmiedel, for example, who making a bad use of the legal doctrine that an admission against one's interest is a conclusive presump-

tion of truth, and taking as his supreme canon of criticism that whatever is said in favor of Jesus is to be accounted for as expressing the partiality of his friends or regarded as an interpolation by a later hand, tries to throw doubt upon every element of supernaturalism in the record of his life.

But criticism of this sort leads to absurd conclusions. Of course the praise of an enemy is worth more as evidence than the adulation of a friend. But were the enemies of Jesus writing his biography, and could you expect his friends to refuse to say what was true of him lest a later critic should discredit it on the ground of partiality? Is Boswell a discredited biographer because he had kindly feelings toward Dr. Johnson? Schmiedel however, with his critical postulate in his hand, proceeds to make a solitude of the whole landscape of early Christian history, and as we look across the plain in the light of what according to his arbitrary treatment of the Gospels must be regarded as the splendid sunset of Christian faith, we see nine rugged pillars standing as the sole reminder of the famous city of Gospel story through whose four quarters once walked the blessed Jesus and where his mighty works were done. One of the nine 'pillar-passages'—to abandon the metaphor—is that which reads, "But of that day and that hour knoweth no man, not even the Son, but the Father," and that is allowed to remain as a truthful element in the Gospel story because it seems to be adverse to the Saviour's claims. This is one specimen of criticism, and here is another.

3. There is a class of critics who are known as eschatologists, because they devote their attention to what Jesus has to say concerning the later order of events. These writers do not interpret "the Kingdom of Heaven," after the manner of some, as referring to the Church or to a reign of peace and good will on earth during the life of individuals, as the Ritschlians do. They interpret the Kingdom of Heaven in the terms of certain apocalyptic literature prevalent in Palestine about the time of the Advent. Jesus, they say, thought he was the Messiah, and looked forward to his death as the prelude to the new dispensation, promised to come again in the clouds of heaven with power and great glory and set up a kingdom. Meanwhile, he gave his disciples a code of ethics (interimistic ethics) which were meant to serve the purpose until he came and the new kingdom should be set up wherein men should neither marry nor be given in marriage. In other words, these writers say that Jesus was a fanatic and a man of unbalanced mind. But this is a gratuitous hypothesis which carries to its logical conclusion the idea more euphemistically expressed by Professor Kirsopp Lake.[3]

Let me ask this question, Would any jury of

[3] Kirsopp Lake, *The Stewardship of Faith.*

alienists and psychologists to-day, taking into account the life of Jesus as it is portrayed in the Evangelists and considering the sobriety of his utterances, his humility, his reverence, and the lofty character of his teaching, for one moment entertain such a baseless charge against him? But what can the critics do? Their postulate is that the Incarnation is impossible and they are left to choose, as best they can, between his being a fanatic or a paranoiac. But in either case the conclusion is contradicted in his own personality, and for refutation we need only mark his calm behaviour and unfaltering confidence in his mission; and watch the sharp knife of ethical insight with which he makes a clean cleavage of every moral question into hemispheres of right and wrong.

4. There is still another class of critics who, by a process of exegesis derived from a fancied psychological discernment, are looking for an earlier and simpler form of Christianity back of the one presented in the existing biography of Jesus. But if the mythologists are right, why need we trouble ourselves any further? If the eschatologists are right, why suppose that anything would be gained by seeking in the Gospels for a more primitive form of Christian belief? That men are making the attempt is proof that they have no confidence in the critical results to which reference has been made; and that the class of critics to whom I now ask

your attention are leading a forlorn hope will soon be apparent.[4]

The admissions of these men are worth far more than their theories. Their postulate is, I say again, that Jesus was only a man, and that the Incarnation was impossible. And yet the Gospels, and not the Gospels only but the whole New Testament, proclaim the belief that Jesus was both God and man. There must therefore have been a gospel earlier than those which we have: that is to say, a primitive conception of Jesus as only a man, and they are looking for that earlier belief. That they are looking for it is evidence that upon the Gospels as we have them no honest construction can be put other than that which is the common faith of Christendom. To find trace of this earlier Gospel these critics scrutinize verses, sift every word, and with an ingenuity worthy of a better cause, search as for hid treasure for hints of an earlier and purely human view of Jesus; but with poor result. The nearest approach they have made is the supposition —childish as it seems to me—that the Evangelists, who had been led by belief in his Resurrection to regard Jesus as a divine person, had been so accustomed to regard him as simply a human being that they sometimes inadvertently spoke of him as such. In other words, the theory is that instead of having

[4] See B. B. Warfield, "The Two Natures" and "Recent Christological Speculation," *American Journal of Theology*, June and October, 1911.

two natures, a human and a divine, the Evangelists
being converts to the idea of his divinity addressed
him as a human being after they were convinced
that he was Divine; very much, I suppose, as having known a certain person as Miss Brown, I sometimes inadvertently called her by her maiden name
after she became Mrs. Jones. Surely this is very
shallow reasoning. The attempt to get rid of the
two natures in the person of Christ is a ridiculous
failure, and the only contribution Dr. Johannes
Weiss has made to theological science is the admission—implied in the object of his search—that the
Evangelists who had intimately known the human
Jesus believed that he was also divine. So ends
the long chapter of destructive criticism. What
new forms it may yet assume, or is assuming, I do
not pretend to know. But for the present at least
the great storm seems to be over, save for a few
retreating clouds, subdued thunder on the horizon,
and now and then a pale flash of lightning, all of
them signs of clearing weather.

But not all of the students of modern Christology are like those to whom attention has been given.
There are those who reveal a tendency to go back
to the decisions at Chalcedon. It was a step in the
right direction when the old mythical theory refuted itself by the vindication of the early origin
of the New Testament books; another step when
the latest mythical theory divides the critics into
those who believe that primitive Christianity was

most of the difficulties which men feel in religion are complicated with those concerning a theory of the universe. It is the foregone conclusion of a mechanically constituted world that seems to condition all other beliefs; and so men fly from one subject to another and if you talk with them about the divinity of Christ they will turn back to the book of Genesis and ask your opinion about the cosmogony, the origin of species and the creation of man. It is with them as if you were to ask a boy how he is getting on with his Livy, and he should say, 'Oh yes, I know all about Romulus and Remus, but that preface is a pretty tough bit of Latin. I have hard work to know what Livy means when he says: *Facturusne operae pretium sim . . . . nec satis scio, nec, si sciam, dicere ausim.*' You would say: 'It is pretty tough, but go on with the story and come back to that later. Go on by and by to the twenty-first book and read about Hannibal and the second Punic War.' This is what is the matter with a great many people. They are worrying over the preface to the Bible instead of getting at the heart of it which deals with the person and work of Christ. Let us come to that matter now.

iii

The Divinity of Christ

The old Arian position need not be considered. It has played no very important part in the later history of the Church. It has no support in Scripture. It has in it too much supernaturalism to suit those who hold a uniformitarian view of nature. It has too little to meet the moral needs of mankind. To accept the Arian doctrine would only be to accept a supernaturalism that would leave no excuse for refusing to accept the full doctrine of the Divinity of Christ. Besides, it would serve no moral purpose. Jesus would be no example for us and could not take our place under the law. Being himself neither God nor man, he could not fulfil the function of either prophet or priest attributed to him in the New Testament. The issue is clear. Christ is either a man only or else he is both God and man. Let us consider the first alternative.

Jesus was a man. He taught 'paternal theism' and gave us the loftiest conception of duty the world has ever seen. Believing this, we may, in our admiration of his character and teaching, be able to lift our morality up to the level of religion and find in the ethics of Jesus the realization of Matthew Arnold's definition of religion as "morality touched with emotion;" but if a religion like this had anything to say about the life to come, it could say nothing that would be satisfactory. It might say, 'Live according to the teachings of Jesus and all will be well.' But who will, who does, who can, live according to the teachings of Jesus? You may say, 'Be good and you will be happy.' But what does this mean? The better you are, the worse you

suming the doctrine of the infallible contents of the Scriptures, the Divinity of Christ admits of no doubt. This is the method adopted by Liddon in his wonderful Bampton Lectures on the Divinity of Christ. But does the Divinity of Christ rest exclusively on a doctrine of the inspiration of the Scriptures? In order to convince men of the one doctrine must you first prove to them the other? The method I have described may be called the dogmatic method and, conceding the doctrine of the inspiration of the Scriptures, is conclusive. But are we shut up to this method? No; for there is what may be called the apologetic method, and this is the one I am following. The difference may be indicated by an illustration.

A man visiting me at my house asks me how he can get to the city of Hamilton; and someone says, 'Walk about a mile or a mile and a half eastward and you will find a boat.' I say, 'That is quite correct but there is a shorter way, for you need only go down to the foot of the hill and you will find a ferry there.' It is by this ferry that I propose to take you across. But some will say that I am minimizing the importance of the inspiration of the Scriptures. Well, let them. They will say that if one cannot believe in the plenary inspiration of the Scriptures, we may as well give up our Christianity. Then all I have to say is that they are very foolish people. For as I have already shown you, if you can satisfy yourself of the Divinity of Christ without the doctrine of inspiration, how much more can you do so with it! But what am I to do? Must I wait until a man is convinced that the Scriptures are infallible before I begin to talk with him about the Saviour? Surely not. And you must remember that it is easier to prove to some people that the Scriptures teach the Divinity of Christ than it is to prove out of the Scriptures the doctrine of their inspiration. But inspiration or no inspiration, the Scriptures satisfy me that Christ is the incarnate Son of God, and that is what I shall try to show.

1. SPECIFIC PROOFS OF THE DIVINITY OF CHRIST.

(1) *The primitive Christian community believed in the Divinity of Christ.* Were they deluded or mistaken? They had nothing to gain by being parties to a fraud. They saw Jesus, they knew him. They left their fishing nets to follow him. They were in daily fellowship with him. They saw his mighty works and heard his wondrous words. They witnessed his crucifixion, and saw him after his resurrection, and preached that doctrine "beginning at Jerusalem." They did not go to a foreign land where Jesus was unknown. But in Jerusalem, where some of his mighty works were done, where he was crucified, in sight of the high priest's palace, and under the shadow of Pilate's judgment hall they began the work of

time spend the last evening he had with his disciples in building a monument in memory of himself? And so the old question confronts you, What will ye do with this Jesus who is called Christ? Will you say with some, He is a good man; or with others, Nay, but he deceiveth the people?

(4) *There is the evidence furnished in prophecy.* The Old Testament is not a book. It is a literature. As such it has in it all the elements of a great literature: poetry, history, biography, law, story, proverbs, philosophy. Stately, compact, embracing an epoch in a word, it records the coming of the cosmos. Using the common units as the measurement of time, it packs aeons into hours, and makes a week suffice for the world-process from the condensation of the nebulae to the appearance of man upon the planet. Pithy speech serves the writer's end. And so he tells us that God made man in His own image, breathed into him the breath of life, and man became a living soul.

There are gaps in the story of human history, for the Old Testament tale is that of the Chosen People. There is something of prolixity too, for History in her unhasting way stops to tell us stories on the road. But there is method here, for these stories are moral pictures which teach their lessons without argument or exhortation. The value of this mode of instruction men have always known, and it finds its illustration in every Christian home.

For Wisdom dealt with mortal powers,
    Where truth in closest words shall fail,
    When truth embodied in a tale
Shall enter in at lowly doors.

But from the beginning there was a reference to a far-off future the meaning of which became clearer as time went on. Make what you please of the protevangelium, where the promise was that the seed of the woman should bruise the serpent's head. It is hard to understand except an an enigmatical reference to what the New Testament makes plain. Put what construction you please on the theophanies, it will be difficult to separate them from the Messianic idea which comes into more obvious notice as history unfolds. It is not necessary to be inspired in order to prophesy. Fulfilment establishes the truth of the prophecy and vindicates the prophet's claim. Anyone may dream dreams, but it is the inspired man whose dreams come true. And this body of prophecy in which seemingly incompatible attributes were to be united in one man, is such a conspicuous element in the Psalms and in the Prophets that the correspondence of Jesus to these prophecies must arrest attention. How do you explain this correspondence? Some say that men fitted the prophecies to Jesus. What do they mean? Do they regard the Old Testament as a department store where anyone can be fitted to a set of attributes suited to his age, height, and measurement? Was there ever a man who fulfilled

his flesh to eat if he chose. I daresay he himself felt that it was a hard saying. I imagine that Peter paused a moment, and then, forth from his lips came the great *apologia* of Christianity: "Lord, to whom shall we go? thou hast the words of eternal life. And we believe and are sure that thou art that Christ, the Son of the living God."

Does the resurrection of Christ give you trouble? What then do you think of the other arguments? Perhaps you can reach the divinity of Christ by another road, and if you can get there by way of his miracles, his claims, the witness of Paul, or the testimony of the Old Testament, the next time you come up against that 'road-roller' you will not balk at it, for you will say: 'I may not believe in the resurrection of mere man, but Jesus being the man he was, it is not possible that he should be holden of death.' I believe in the resurrection of Christ. Jesus said, "Destroy this temple, and in three days I will raise it up." They took him at his word. He was as good as his word. The morning of the third day saw an empty grave, and it is upon this corner stone of resurrection fact that men have built the cathedral of Christian faith. We have the best of reasons for believing in the resurrection of Jesus, for the women saw him and Peter saw him, and later on Thomas saw him, and his obstinate scepticism, rewarded by the sight of the spear thrust and the print of the nails, gave place to the loyal avowal of his belief in the Deity of Christ.

THE PERSON OF CHRIST

Jr That is True.

The resurrection of Christ is worth more than any miracle recorded in Scripture. It is better attested than any other, more depends upon it than upon any other. It was Paul's vision of the risen Christ that made a preacher out of a persecutor. The Easter faith is the corner stone of Christian apologetics. Men became Christians because they believed that Christ rose from the dead. Men were exhorted by the apostles to become Christians because Christ rose from the dead. If Christ did not rise from the dead, then we have to face the fact that the spread of Christianity was due to belief in an occurrence which never took place. The apostle Paul was in no doubt as to the primacy of Christ's resurrection in the evidences of Christianity. "If Christ be not risen," he says, "then is our preaching vain, and your faith is also vain. Yea, and we are found false witnesses of God, because we have testified of God that he raised up Christ: whom he raised not up, if so be that the dead rise not."

2. THE INTERDEPENDENCE OF THE DOCTRINES OF SCRIPTURE. This is another argument for the Divinity of Christ. If we believe in the resurrection of Christ, we shall see that this throws a sidelight upon the inspiration of the Old Testament, for the fact that Jesus rose from the dead shows that the Incarnation was what the Old Testament was looking forward to, and for which it was a preparation. The resurrection was thus not

[241]

only a proof of the divinity of Christ but a witness to the authority of the Old Testament and thus accomplished a double purpose. Directly it bore witness to our Lord's Divinity, indirectly it gave testimony to the inspiration of the Old Testament and reminds us of the knight's move on the chess-board—one square forward and one square diagonally.

If we believe in the Divinity of Christ we shall have less difficulty in believing in the inspiration of the Old Testament which testified of Christ, and in advance of his coming proclaimed his royalty; for the radiance streaming from the Cross is not like the headlight of a locomotive that illuminates only the track in front of it: it sheds a new light upon the whole of history behind it. Moreover, if Christ is divine, we shall have no difficulty in believing in an expiatory atonement, for we shall be forced to believe that only a great moral crisis in the history of mankind could have been the occasion of his coming in the flesh. All these doctrines stand or fall together. Each helps the other. Let no one say that this is reasoning in a circle. That is an easy and very common allegation, often made without much consideration. Each doctrine supported by its own separate evidence helps to strengthen others that follow from it by logical consequence. It is fallacious, of course, to reason in a circle; but it is foolish to suppose that we must always reason in a straight line. We argue back-

[242]

wards and forwards. We say this is true because that is true. But we also go back to something else that in the strength of its own evidence we also believe to be true, and we say the congruity between the two truths supported separately by adequate testimony, is an additional argument in favor of both of the truths which stand in the relation of congruity to each other. The reasoning reminds one of a train of cars going over a mountain with an engine at each end; so that each car pulls the one behind it and pushes the one in front of it. That is the way I like to look at the matter under discussion, and so I feel perfectly safe in taking my way over the high places of religious thought with the push and pull of separate units of belief.

3. THE CUMULATIVE POWER OF THE ARGUMENTS FOR THE DIVINITY OF CHRIST. We are not shut up to any one line of thought. You may not think that any one of these arguments is absolutely conclusive, but it is hard to resist the cumulative effect of them when they are brought together. Let me make use of a familiar illustration. There is all the difference in the world between the strength of a chain and the strength of a rope. The strength of a chain is the strength of its weakest link. Break one of these links and the chain is useless. But it is not so with a rope. You can break any one of the strands that compose the rope, but when you put them all together it will hold

the biggest ship to her moorings. And what I want to say is that cogent as any one of the arguments for the Divinity of our Lord may be, the cumulative force of them all is greater than the force of any one of them. We have not been carried about by every wind of doctrine. We have a great hope, as an anchor to the soul which entereth into that within the vail. That anchor will hold and the cable which connects us with it will hold. It is not a chain with here and there a worn or rusty link. It is a hawser that will bid defiance to wind and tide. Let us then "hold fast to the profession of our faith," being assured that "we have not followed cunningly devised fables."

iv

Cosmic Effect of the Incarnation.

It must be remembered that as the result of the Incarnation a change has taken place in the economic relations of the Holy Trinity in virtue of which a human being became a partner with God the Father in the affairs of the universe. Jesus has ascended up far above all principalities and powers that he may fill all things and the promise is that he will reconcile all things to himself. Just what this 'anakephalaiosis' means we do not know, but it points to a cosmic significance which may well fill us with wonder. Think of Christ's place as the Divine-man in the great programme of the universe, think of the exalted place which man holds in the thought of God, and compare it for dignity, splendour, and sublimity with any view of the world that the wit of man has devised.

"Forasmuch as the children are partakers of flesh and blood, he also himself took part of the same, for which cause he is not ashamed to call us brethren." We belong therefore to the blood-royal of the universe. In my first lecture I spoke of the theistic view of the world, but we have now come to what we must call the Christian view of the world, and what it means we can better understand by comparing it with another so-called Christian world-view. The Ritschlians have what they call a Christian world-view. But what is it compared with the outlook on the universe given us in the Pauline epistles? They have abandoned metaphysics in theology and yet they speak of the purpose of God. They speak of the kingdom of God, but what a parochial affair it is compared with the gospel as Paul understood it! They may or they may not believe in a future state. There is a tendency among them to call it in question. Their programme has the promise of the life that now is, but is reticent regarding the life beyond the grave. Their hope is in the higher self-realization of successive generations in the present life, but it has little to say regarding the life to come. Their system teaches the Fatherhood of God and the brotherhood of man, but the future for the individual is

be between the academic Malthusian and the military chief, and the issue will be between mouths to feed and soldiers to fight. Decaying nations will face the two evils of a lessening birth-rate and an increasing mortality, and despairing statesmen will find themselves

> Wandering between two worlds, one dead,
> The other powerless to be born.

I know that men will tell us how nature tends to cure the evils of which I speak, and that population automatically diminishes as it increasingly taxes the soil, like the thermostat, I suppose, in our houses which automatically shuts off the heat when it rises above seventy degrees and turns it on when it falls below sixty. This is a problem which of course has but little practical application to the present generation and will be interesting mainly to those who take a long speculative look ahead. But the time may come when war will be regarded as one of the world's best friends and men will feel that military honours for those who survive the battles, and tablets to the memory of the heroic dead, will be a cheap way of keeping the fruits of the earth for those who are best fitted to enjoy them. To keep the peace in this present world we need morality; to keep morality we need faith in the life to come. We must have a cosmic interest in life to protect the interests of this planetary parish in which we live. It is the Gospel which gives us this cosmic view of life. It is Christ who has stretched our interest in mankind until it reaches what Lucretius calls the "flaming ramparts of the world."

v

THE INCARNATION AND IMMORTALITY

But the need of an immortal life as a basis of morality is after all a less important thing than the fact of immortality itself. There are men perhaps who if the choice were left to them would prefer that death should end all. If they were only certain that it does, they would not complain. But they cannot be certain, and though they may persuade themselves that immortality is a dream, their persuasion has no support. And if there were no immortality, men might say that dying by thousands as men do, it only means that the individual dies in the company of his fellows. But this is not the case. Every man has to take the same lonely journey, and it is the uncompanioned loneliness of death that accounts for much of its terror. Moreover, though we were reconciled to the loss of immortality, we might still retain our sense of obligation, and our clear discrimination between right and wrong. We know that there are men possessed of the highest sense of duty who have lost faith in a future state. Truth would still mean something to men even though there were no belief in anything beyond the bound of life. This sense of moral obligation undoubtedly has survival value for the race, but this is no guarantee of its own survivorship. And it is to be feared that with a universal feeling that as the brute dieth so dieth man, our race would soon reach the brute's level of morality.

But immortality is not a gift that one may accept or refuse at pleasure. If we accept Christianity we must believe in another world and that immortality is a destiny. If we are to believe Christianity we are to believe that not only the fact of immortality but the kind of immortality, and the conditions for the enjoyment of that kind of immortality, are revealed to us in the Person and work of Christ. He it is who has brought life and immortality to light. Nothing can be more conspicuous in the New Testament than that whatever part a man has in determining his own destiny, an immortality of some kind is his destiny. The Christian faith is that Christ has achieved for us the opportunity of a happy hereafter. Whether or no there are any conditions connected with that hereafter, the Bible speaks confidently of "the inheritance of the saints in light."

The great achievement of Christianity is the bringing in of an eternal hope. If that hope is justified, then surely the man who pretends to be an exponent and a teacher of Christianity is guilty of criminal neglect if he is reticent regarding it. If a minister of the Gospel is entrusted with the duty of telling men about the future life and the conditions annexed to its enjoyment, he is certainly culpable if he allows men to believe that a life of moral respectability and a reasonable amount of enjoyment are all that he can look forward to. But this is what some men are doing. They are acting as a man might, who being made the trustee of an estate and charged under the will of the testator to give the income of it to the legatees during the time of their residence in their present place of abode, but in the event of their emigrating to a foreign land, to turn over to them the *corpus* of the estate, should say he knew nothing of the country to which they were going, nothing of its laws of inheritance, and was unable to enter into negotiations with that country; he had done what he regarded as the next best and had paid over to the heirs the whole estate before they set sail, so that there was now nothing coming to them in the strange land whither they had gone.

It is this emigrating clause in our Father's will that interests us here. So much is allowed us as his legatees during our life in the land of our birth, the residue to be given after our emigration. My fellow trustees, is it fair to these legatees, heirs of God and joint heirs with Christ to an inheritance incorruptible, undefiled, and that fadeth not away, not to tell them what is coming to them? Do you think it fair not to let them know, moreover, that by a provision in our Father's will, they may forfeit that inheritance for lack of compliance with its conditions? Do you think you can give a satisfactory account of your stewardship by pleading as justification of your action the flimsy *si pres* doctrine to which I have referred?

It is not so long ago that it used to be said to impoverished families in the crowded countries of Europe, 'Emigrate,' and to the ambitious youth without fortune but possessed of rugged health, 'Go west, young man.' For reasons that are familiar to us there are restrictions now imposed upon the entrance of the alien within our gates. But men are emigrating notwithstanding. They are 'going west' in more senses than one—hundreds every minute, thousands every week, hundreds of thousands every month, millions every year. They are going, but whither they do not know. What are we for? What is the Church for? Mainly to help these emigrants. What should we do? Tell them how to seek a country, even an heavenly; tell them where to look for a city whose builder and maker is God; tell them of the land that is fairer than day; tell them of Jerusalem the Golden, of "the light that hath no evening, the health that hath no sore." Dispel from their minds the terrors of the voyage. Tell them that they will not be aliens or strangers there, but fellow citizens of the saints and of the household of God; that their quota will never be filled as long as there is one who desires to enter that land of plenty; that they need no money as the price of their landing; that they need fear no doubtful inspection, for the Lord knoweth them that are his; that there is no house of detention there, whether they call it purgatory or paradise; that there is no night there, and no more death.

Sermon Subject "Emigration"

measure, for he was great in each of the three mental dimensions.

1. INTELLECT. Whatever else Paul might have been, he could never have appeared except as a man of very unusual intellect. Whether he was acquainted with the philosophical speculations of the schools is a matter of which we have no information further than that he knew, as we do in our day, the injurious effect of philosophic speculation. The reason of this is plain enough; for the subjects with which philosophy deals are precisely those which fall within the purview of the inspired writers, and the unwillingness of men to correct their speculative philosophy by the teachings of revelation is no new thought with us, as it was no passing phase of opinion in the days of the apostles. But whatever degree of acquaintance Paul had with the answer of philosophy to the problems of the speculative intellect, no one can doubt that he knew what the problems were. He had clear convictions with respect to God's relation to the world, but his sense of the intimacy of God with his works did not lower his conception of the divine personality, nor did his belief in the latter doctrine prevent him from expressing himself in terms which, taken by themselves, might well be compared to some of the pantheistic utterances of later men.

The antinomies and apparent contradictions with which philosophy has made us familiar were not novelties to Paul. Had one said to him that the world itself is a manifestation of God he would not have demurred, for he has said substantially the same thing more than once. Had he been told that the phenomenal world does not give us an exact account of the noumenal world, he need only quote in support of this position his own words to the effect that the things which are seen are temporal but the things which are unseen are eternal. He had uncompromising views of human duty; but he also had views quite as uncompromising respecting the divine purpose. His figure of the clay and the potter, which Matthew Arnold regarded as an unmistakable lapse into Calvinism, would in no sense have led him to qualify his doctrine of moral obligation. And when men said, as they did say, "Why doth he yet find fault? for who hath resisted his will?" Paul answered "Nay but, O man, who art thou that repliest against God?" This, by the way, only shows that the objections to the Calvinistic theology which are made now, were made against the teaching of Paul, but without shaking his confidence in the divine purpose; and we may add, without any need of their shaking ours. The conflict between the flesh and the spirit which is a great moral antinomy, was never more clearly stated, so Edward Caird admits, than by the apostle Paul; yet he made no attempt to reconcile the two nor did he find in this conflict any excuse for the men who felt the force of it. We may safely say that the questions in regard to God's relation to the

wrecked and the soldiers began to think of their own lives. They were Roman soldiers, but not like those on the 'Birkenhead.' They wanted to kill the prisoners, but the officer in command stopped them, out of regard for Paul. Then came the command, 'overboard every man who can swim.' This done, the rest—some on boards and some on broken pieces of the ship—got safely to land. Paul was not a man who could be kept in obscurity. Prisoner as he was, when the crisis came his was the controlling voice.

But of course this incident was out of the sphere of Paul's ordinary activities. He was pre-eminently a servant of Christ. He seems to have combined the duties of the local missionary with those of the Secretary of the Board of Foreign Missions of the primitive Church. He visited the churches, but he founded them too. And he did this without forgetting the claims of home missions, for wherever he went he took up a collection for the poor saints at Jerusalem. But perhaps nothing in Paul's life, outside of his letters, was greater than his statesmanship. The crisis was sure to come. He could not preach justification by faith and at the same time insist on circumcision. The two were incompatible. The question was whether Christianity was just Judaism with a revised confession of faith, or whether it was a new dispensation. It was whether they were going to have two churches, one for Gentiles and one for Jews, whether they were to stand by the logical consequences of justification by faith, or remain to all intents and purposes Jews. Paul is the exponent of justification by faith. He taught it, and reasoned it out in the epistle to the Romans. It is a treatise. But the Galatian epistle is a polemic. 'If you insist on circumcising these Gentile converts, you have fallen from grace and Christ will profit you nothing.' That was Paul's position. He had had a controversy with Peter on this subject. He was Peter's junior. He had come into the band of apostles at a later date. Peter had been prominent among the disciples, their leader in fact. But Paul "withstood him to the face, because he was to be blamed." Probably Peter felt hurt and thought Paul was a meddlesome innovator. But Paul persevered and his logic carried the day. The epistle to the Galatians is a treatise on justification—in that light Luther regarded it; but it is more than that; it may be called a great state paper. It is Christianity's declaration of independence. It was an intimation that these colonial churches would not take orders from Jerusalem. It asserted the liberty under which Christ has made us free. Paul is the hero of Gentile Christianity.

But now we come to another phase of the will. The will is the mind's executive, but it has to do with theory also. Paul was a moralist. He was a man who had thought through the problem of duty. His ethics hold such a prominent place in

impression. An idol was nothing, and the wine was not made unfit for consumption, nor was it wrong to use it, because it had been offered to the idol; but its use might serve to compromise a Christian believer and give rise to the belief that he had taken part in the worship of idols. Perfectly right in itself, an act may be wrong in its influence. "Let not your good be evil spoken of." Abstain, rather than offend the conscience of the weak brethren. The weak brother, however, may put too much burden on the individual who feels perfectly justified in what he does. Paul's conclusion was that there is an area of conduct in regard to which every man must be his own judge, be fully persuaded in his own mind; and within that area no man has a right to interfere. This doctrine of expediency clearly puts a man on his own responsibility to be governed by his own conscience. One naturally compares it with the act of a man steering his own ship. But it would be a closer parallel if we conceive of the man as the ship and the ship as steering herself. Not long since I learned how to make a better use of this nautical figure. On a voyage to New York my friend the captain invited me to come up to the bridge and see his new quartermaster. I went, and when I got there no one was at the wheel; the ship was steering herself. By means of an attachment of the gyroscopic compass to the steering gear it was only necessary when the ship "took her departure" to set the gyroscopic compass to the proper course and the ship would steer herself. That was the best illustration of the autonomy of the conscience I had ever seen. So I said to the captain, 'You do not need the magnetic compass any more?' 'Oh yes we do,' he said, 'for this gyroscopic attachment is a very delicate arrangement and is liable to get out of order; and when it does, we steer by the old magnetic compass.' Better still, I thought, though my mind was not on navigation. It is all very well to talk about the autonomy of the individual conscience. But it, too, is a delicate piece of machinery and it is well to have the old compass within reach. Keep a light in the binnacle therefore so that when occasion calls for it you can read the compass. Your conscience will never supersede the Bible.

3. FEELING. Paul was a thinker and a dialectician; but he was something more than a logic-chopper. He was a man of action; but he was no cold-blooded man of affairs doing what he had to do without depression or enthusiasm. He was a man of deep feeling. His theology had warmth. His practical reason was suffused with emotion. Paul was a mystic. He believed in the presence of God in his soul. His spiritual life was constantly reinforced by the presence of the spirit of God. He took no credit to himself: "Not I, but Christ that dwelleth in me." "The spirit helpeth our infirmities," he said. The Christian graces were the fruits of the spirit; love, joy, peace, long-

suffering, gentleness, goodness, faith, meekness, temperance. Paul's religion was a synthesis of intellect, feeling, and will. Deep conviction, warm feeling, and resolute will, blended under the fusing influence of the spirit, made him the man he was. Paul was not one of those unemotional people whose activities work with the accuracy of a machine which takes in the raw material at one end and turns out the finished product at the other. People of this type do not best represent the Christian life. A little warmth of interest; a little difference of action prompted by the feeling of the moment; a sense of gladness in the doing of a kind act; a little tenderness of feeling evoked by sympathy or love, would lift many a good deed out of the category of machine-made benevolence into the sphere of spontaneous affection. I say this realizing that what is called the personal touch is impossible in connection with the great benevolences of our day which shed such lustre on our present civilization. Still, when you read of what Paul said and did, you will see routine at its lowest and spontaneity at its highest level.

Now it is in the union of these three elements that we find the highest form of religious life. A religion that is all feeling, may lack the coherency of form; a religion that is all thought, is apt to be devoid of zeal; a religion that is all will, misses the guiding hand of conviction and is wanting in the inspiration of feeling. The thinker who has no love for the great hymns of Christendom is deficient in the power that moves the world. *Pectus facit theologum.* The brooding theologian whose spirit is not stirred within him by the sight of men wholly given to the idolatry of gain and pleasure is deficient in an important element of greatness. The great theologian is a man of three mental dimensions. If you wish to see this illustrated read Paul's letters.

How wonderful these letters are: written with extemporaneous facility and freedom; with no effort at studied diction, and evidently with no thought of posthumous publication. There is no carefully prepared outline of thought. The author writes with a running pen; logical argument interrupted with a chiding parenthesis; calm statement abruptly broken with a momentary outburst of indignant feeling. Sometimes the trend of thought is evidently moving toward a climax, and as it proceeds gathers momentum, takes flight, and on the rhythmic wings of cumulative clauses soars to the higher levels of religious enthusiasm. Great passages which live in the memory of us all come sometimes as unexpected episodes in the middle of didactic narrative, as when Paul speaks of the earthly house of this tabernacle being dissolved, or writes the chapter on the resurrection, or his eulogy of love. How tenderly he speaks and how it grieves him even when he seeks to justify himself, that he has hurt the feelings of those to whom he wrote. He writes one letter to the Corinthians that made them sorry; then writes another to tell them that he is sorry that he made them sorry, and yet glad too, for they sorrowed unto repentance. Their sorrow has also something in it that comes back upon himself as he anticipates his next visit to them: "For if I make you sorry, who is he then that maketh me glad, but the same which is made sorry by me?"

This *abandon*, this abrupt, unstudied manner so remote from the style of a thesis or an essay, is apparent even in "the Romans," the most severely logical form of reasoning that he has left us. The prevailing topic of his thought was our freedom from condemnation through the atoning blood of Christ; the blessed hope of a glorious immortality; our complete dependence on divine grace; and the inadequacy of anything that we can do for our own salvation.

Into the nature of the pre-incarnate life of the second person of the Godhead he but seldom ventures save in the epistles to the Ephesians and the Colossians. He taught with unequivocal plainness the doctrine of the second coming of Christ, and this has always been, as it is still, the belief of the Christian Church, though there is what sometimes amounts to an acute difference of opinion among Christians to-day respecting the order of eschatological events connected with the second advent.

Think now of the wonderful tact Paul showed

in the letter to Philemon. What a gentleman he
was! Onesimus of course should return to his master, but what welcome would he meet? The claim
of Philemon was not to be overlooked, but Onesimus had a claim too: the latter on the former,
because he was now a brother in Christian bonds;
the former on the latter, because Onesimus was
still his slave. Read also Paul's First Epistle to
Timothy, exactly such as a minister of experience
would write to a younger man. It breathes affection in every line: in Paul's warning of the apos-
tasies that would come; in his exhortation to dili-
gence in the work of the ministry; in his reference
to Timothy's mother and grandmother, both of
whom were devout believers in the Scriptures; and
in his solicitude for Timothy's health, together
with the prescription he sent him for his often infirmities. Then came the personal references to his
own circumstances. He was lonely—no one but
Luke with him, Luke for aught we know being
perhaps poor company and occupied besides with
his work on the Third Gospel or in making notes
for his forthcoming Acts of the Apostles; Demas
had apostatized; Alexander the coppersmith had
treated him badly—Paul was hurt, angry in fact,
and dismissed the matter with blunt compliments.
Whether the breach was ever healed we do not
know, but I feel confident that Alexander got no
Christmas card from Paul that year when the time
for season's greetings came round. Measure these

letters by any standard you please; compare them with letters of other famous men, from Seneca to Horace Walpole and thence down to those of Walter Page—Paul's will in nowise suffer by comparison. The letters reveal the man: rugged and resolute in his convictions, triumphant in his Christian trust, enthusiastic in his work, rejoicing in the part he took in founding the Christian Church in heathen lands, and confident above all things in reference to the future.

Paul's correspondence shows no self-pity, no complaint that his appeal to Caesar was in vain, no murmuring because his active ministry was stopped by his imprisonment; but exhibits him as rejoicing rather that the things which happened to him had turned out to the furtherance of the Gospel.

And this reminds us too of Paul's speeches. He was evidently a master here, though some seemed not to think so highly of his oratorical gifts as of his letters. Listen to him at Mars' Hill. How differently some men would have acted; Paul might have said, 'You are all polytheists; and worse than that—as though you had not enough gods already, you have actually built an altar to one you never heard of.' But no; Paul, with what Hegel would have called a reconciliation of contradictions, took advantage of the elements of religious faith common to all of them, resolved their differences into a higher unity, and then preached to them about the God whom they ignorantly worshipped and whose offspring they were, aptly quoting one of their own poets in support of his statement. Standing then on the platform of a common theistic faith he preached to them Jesus and the resurrection.

Take his address to the elders at Ephesus. It was an affecting meeting with these men who had come down to the boat to 'see him off.' I can imagine that I see them as they waited there: Paul on the deck, they on the dock. All of them sad, but the elders "sorrowing most of all because they should see his face no more." Paul charged them to feed the Church of God over which the Holy Ghost had made them overseers (episcopoi). They were both prestbyters and bishops, age and office reinforcing each other. And once more, take his great speech before King Agrippa, one of the greatest forensic efforts in literature. This was not the first time Paul had spoken in his own behalf. He had spoken before Felix, and also before Festus, but now he was to stand in the presence of royalty. King Agrippa was on the bench. Queen Bernice was present. It was an occasion of "great pomp." And when the great case was opened, the case which was to be of more importance than any in history save the trial of Jesus, Paul was permitted to speak for himself. Unabashed, calmly but with great dignity, he told the story of his life and recited the circumstances connected with his arrest and imprisonment. To Agrippa's interruption, whether sarcastic or serious, Paul replied with deference. To the challenge of his sanity by Festus he answered with warmth and perhaps a touch of petulance. The result was unfavorable. I think Agrippa might have said: 'If you insist on your appeal to Caesar, of course you must go; but we are quite ready to settle the case here and now.' But he missed his opportunity. These governors were a weak set. They had the Roman formulas of justice by heart, but they did not have the sense of justice in their souls. Pilate was weak. He found no fault in Jesus, but turned him over to the Jewish Sanhedrim. Felix was weak, and as his term of office was expiring deemed it best to leave Paul's case as a legacy to his successor. Festus was weak, and preferred to have the case tried before King Agrippa. And Agrippa was weak. *Sotto voce* he said to Festus, "This man might have been set at liberty if he had not appealed to Caesar." Why then did he not set him at liberty?

And so Paul went as a prisoner to Rome there to end his days as a martyr, but not until he had preached the gospel for two whole years in his own hired house, thus finishing his missionary career in the capital of the Roman empire, and saying in one of his latest utterances, "Salvation is unto the Gentiles." This is the man who under God was to be the great interpreter of Christianity to the world. To that interpretation, let us now turn.

ii

PAUL THE THEOLOGIAN

Paul entered into no discussion in regard to the doctrine of the Trinity though it was either expressed or implied throughout his writings. Nor did he discuss the questions in regard to the Person of Christ which were afterwards dealt with at the Council of Chalcedon, but there can be no doubt as to his belief in the divinity of Christ; and the themes to which he devoted himself would have been without meaning on any other view than that Christ was God. The theology of Paul turned on the question of sin and the remedy for it. We may almost say that Paul had but one great theme and that was sin and salvation. Let us turn our attention to this.

1. SIN. No writer in the New Testament is so full and explicit in his interpretation of the origin, meaning, and consequences of sin as is Paul. We need go no further than our own individual experience to find that there is something wrong with us: something in us that meets rebuke from our fellow men and in the voice of our own consciences. Do what we will, it is hard for us to escape reproach or blame in some form. We are hedged about by prohibitions that interrupt our pleasure and prevent us from following out our inclinations. If a bit of pathway in front of us seems inviting we have no sooner begun our walk

than we read the notice, "No road this way." If our inclination takes us in another direction we are informed that trespassing is forbidden. If we see a spreading tree where shade invites repose we have no sooner moved in its direction than we are told to "keep off the grass."

Why are such inhibitions put upon our natural inclinations? You do not blame the brutes because they have the lust of the flesh. On the contrary Walt Whitman, if my memory is correct, seems to admire those 'dumb driven cattle' because they seem contented and are not always thinking of their sins. And there are some people who make excuses for wrong-doing on the ground that such wrong-doing is natural. But why should it be wrong to do what nature prompts us to do? Nature prompts a man to steal. Why then find fault with him for stealing? Man seems to be the only animal whose natural impulses are the subject of fault finding. There is evidently something wrong with him. What is it? A large part of Paul's writing is given to the answering of this question. You may say that man is selfish. Yes; but why should he not be selfish? On naturalistic principles you have nothing to say. It is his nature to be selfish. Being selfish, he steals. Being selfish, he protects his stolen goods by laws which punish theft. Being selfish, he finds that it pays to be benevolent, and he encourages unselfishness from selfish motives, and the same selfishness which once encouraged robbery and murder now follows a policy of peace and good will.

This seems to be an inadequate solution of our problem. Paul said we have all sinned and come short of the glory of God. He also said that sin is the transgression of the law. But men have found an excuse for sin even with this definition of it. The inclination to do wrong calls for effort to resist it. All these temptations, the lust of the flesh, the lust of the eye, and the pride of life, constitute a moral gymnasium. They are like dumb-bells, or parallel bars, which serve to tone up our moral nature and make us 'fit.' If virtue were an appetite there would be no merit in upright conduct. No man is commended for eating when he is hungry or drinking when he is thirsty as though it were a meritorious achievement. In this way men have come to regard sin as serving a great moral purpose in the world so that our evil appetites and passions have this to recommend them, that they help to set us up in moral fibre. Then a man might encourage his appetites just for the sake of resisting them, in short, might do evil that good may come. Some act on this principle to their ruin. The question with some seems to be whether sin is sinful. Paul had no doubt on this point; and is at pains to show us "the exceeding sinfulness of sin." He went further. He not only tells us that we are under a law which we are bound to obey but that we are under a law which we cannot obey.

He taught us that men are dead in trespasses and sins.

You may think Paul's logic repulsive, but it is not shallow. It is a logic which not only holds us guilty for what we fail to do, but for our inability to do otherwise. He tells us that we are suffering from a hereditary malady which is both a disease and a crime, that the fathers have eaten sour grapes and the children's teeth have been set on edge, that you cannot blame a tree for bearing sour fruit unless you can blame it for being a sour tree. It is the evil tree that bears evil fruit as Jesus said, and the good tree which bears good fruit. And so, regard it under the idea of imputation, generic oneness, or heredity, as you please, Paul leads us back to the representative responsibility involved in the Adamic relationship. I am not saying that the view presented is the only possible view of sin. I am saying that it is the only Biblical view of sin.

I can conceive of another view that is in no sense naturalistic; that, in fact, is in full keeping with a theistic view of the world. A man may quite willingly admit that his ideals forbid his self-contentment and that his self-condemnation is a witness to a higher life; that the evil conditions which have generated laws favoring a nobler morality have worked together for a higher and ultimate good; that pain, sorrow, suffering, have been 'steps up to heaven'; that the race's advance to higher ideals bears witness to God's presence in the soul;

and that a man may rationally put an optimistic construction upon all of life, and in spite of sorrow, suffering and sin be able to say:

Still all my song shall be
Nearer, my God, to Thee,
Nearer to Thee.

This is not by any means an irrational idea. But it is not Christian. Salvation does not mean accelerated growth. It does not mean fertilizing the plant to help its development, nor pruning the vine that it may bring forth more fruit. These elements enter into the growth of Christian experience; but the root ideas of salvation are something very different. It is easy to represent humanity as a family of children who are undergoing a process of training, and are moving on from little to more, with an ideal perfection before them as the goal of achievement. But this is not Paul's idea at all. According to the Pauline doctrine God is dealing with an "apostate race".

2. SALVATION. Having considered sin we must consider also the consequences of sin. The Bible treats this matter with unmistakable plainness. It has a great deal to say in regard to the penalty of sin. In order to have a better understanding of this, it may be profitable for us to consider for a moment the philosophy of punishment under the operation of human law. There are three views as to the ends to be served by penal enactments in

criminal jurisprudence: they may be considered as emendatory, preventive, or retributive. These views are not to be regarded as exclusive in the sense that the adoption of one leaves no room for the other two, since there is a proper place for each. A parent chastises his child for the good of the child, and does it at the great cost of his own feelings. He may be overindulgent and spoil the child by sparing the rod, or by extreme harshness he may alienate the child's affections. The infliction of punishment should always be a mixture of justice and love, and neither should be sacrificed in the interest of the other. Nor should the idea of correction or prevention blind the parent to the fact of ill-desert which underlies all penalty.

That punishment has moral improvement as its end is holding a very prominent place in penology at the present time, and there is much to be said in its favor. Imprisonment opens a door of opportunity for the moral improvement of the criminal and we should take advantage of it. But it is a mistake to regard moral improvement as its end. For unless the criminal has done something that deserves punishment his imprisonment is a violation of his rights. It is always easy to go to extremes. There are those who have carried the emendatory idea of punishment so far that one wonders sometimes how the sentence of a year in prison for one can act as a deterrent for others, in view of the consideration with which the prisoner is treated and the unwonted kindnesses of which he is the recipient. Two things tend to blunt the sense of ill-desert in the minds of men who consider this matter. There is the natural sentiment of human sympathy, which sometimes takes the form of ill-advised sentimentality. This is sometimes carried so far that the criminal may truly say:

> Stone walls do not a prison make,
> Nor iron bars a cage—

such pity do men show for one whose lot is "hard labour and jail fare." Far be it from me to complain of the disinterested kindness to the criminal on the part of those who visit him in prison, serve him with luxuries, and supply him with flowers. But when they thus seek to divert him from the consciousness of wrong-doing, they mistake the true end of punishment and are undertaking the impossible task of securing salvation by sympathy.

Then, too, there is the prevailing feeling, which in its popular form outruns scientific induction, that all wrong-doing is due to some physical abnormality, that therefore imprisonment will work no cure and that the prisoner's only chance for social salvation is in psychiatry or surgery. And here again I am only uttering a caution, lest what is best in some cases should be regarded as the proper treatment of all.

Besides the emendatory theory of punishment

there is the preventive theory, enunciated by the English judge who said, "We punish men not for stealing goods, but that goods may not be stolen." To this view also I demur, for if stealing is not a wrong that demands punishment it is an act of injustice to the thief to imprison him simply as a warning to others. But conceding even that prevention is the end of punishment, the inference may easily be reached that in order to make it a terror to evil-doers we must be deaf to the voice of sympathy, and the logical effect of this would be a relapse into the cruelties of prison life which have been thrillingly exposed in song and story.

These two views of punishment may easily become contradictory; for if you make prison life attractive you destroy its deterrent effect, and if you seek to enhance the deterrent effect you run into cruelty. It is indeed safe to say that unless the three ideas already referred to are kept in view in the administration of justice, there will be a collapse of justice in the act of administering it, and we shall have either a system of love without law or of law without love.

Turning now to the consideration of the Pauline idea of salvation, we find in its provisions the supreme example of the union of two seemingly conflicting conceptions, law and love. It presents itself in three aspects as something done for us, something done in us, and something that we must do.

(1) *The Objective Side of Salvation.* The Pauline statement of the case is very simple and can be easily understood. Sin has separated us from God; there is alienation. Sin has exposed us to penalties; there is punishment. The estrangement must give place to reconciliation. Paul represents the method of reconciliation by the use of three figures of speech borrowed respectively from the court, the camp, and the altar. We are insolvent debtors, but Christ has settled the claim against us. We have been carried captive by our sin, but Christ has paid the price of our ransom. We have offended against God's holy laws, but Christ is the propitiation for our sins.

These teachings of Scripture need no explanation. They shine in their own light. But men have allowed their attitude to human law to affect their theological convictions. They say, 'We cannot believe in a retributive punishment on the part of God which we are giving up in regard to men.' They tell us that either we have put a wrong interpretation on the Scriptures, or that they cannot believe the Scriptures when they teach a view of punishment which they are repudiating. They say that if God deals with men as they would not deal with a criminal then they are better than God. And so, advancing from a negation of belief to positive criticisms of the Almighty, they take Pope's ridicule seriously when he tells us to

Snatch from his hand the balance and the rod,
Re-judge his justice, be the God of God.

But these men do not see that the salvation spoken of in the New Testament is in strict accord with our instinctive conceptions of penalty; that it is an uncompromising union of justice and love; and that it goes beyond the wildest dream of the legal reformer in that it offers a pardon to every criminal, provides a cure for every spiritual ailment, and turns the penal consequences of sin into agents in man's moral improvement.

But when men abandon belief in the retributive justice of God, they give up the strongest reason for the incarnation; and when this reason ceases to have weight with them, belief in the incarnation will not long survive. Deprived of the hope which this belief inspires, they are left to find what comfort they can in their own merits or the mercy of God. They may elect to place themselves under the care of Nature which shows no favours and knows no forbearance; or trust to the indulgence of a Father who is too blind to see and too fond to punish the errors of his children. But in either case they are acting in opposition to the only authoritative information that has ever reached us. To give up the doctrine of retribution is to abandon the elements of Christianity which give it worth. The man who denies the doctrine of Christ's atonement is left without gratitude, for he is robbed of the joy of his salvation; without penitence, for he no longer feels the quickened sense of sin which belief in the atonement promotes; without a sense of security in reference to the future, for he has given up the only basis on which that security can rest. He is dumb in the presence of the words which tell him that Christ was "made sin for us, who knew no sin, that we might be made the righteousness of God in him"; he is speechless when he fain would say, 'I am persuaded that nothing shall separate me from the love of God which is in Christ Jesus my Lord'; and the whole trend of New Testament teaching stands meaningless before him, for he has lost faith in everything which pertains to God's great adventure in taking on himself a human nature to save the blessed destinies of mankind.

(2) *The Subjective Side of Salvation*. There is something to be done in us. We sin because we have a sinful nature. That nature must be changed. Jesus said to Nicodemus, Ye must be born again. Nicodemus did not understand that Jesus was speaking metaphorically, and therefore put a literal interpretation upon his word. Christ was using an analogy which Nicodemus did not comprehend. The reality referred to pertained to a sphere that transcended experience and our Lord said: 'If I speak in the terms of human experience and you fail to apprehend my meaning, how would the matter be made plainer if I spoke of heavenly things?' It was a lesson of far-reaching signifi-

cance and has a wide application. It was the doctrine of regeneration of which our Lord was speaking. Men differ in respect to the way that regeneration comes. But whether we receive it by sacramental grace, sufficient grace, or efficacious grace, it is the accepted doctrine of Christianity that we need it.

Our nature puts limits on our powers. Your child has no ear for music, but you wish her to have a musical education. She practises industriously, and gets but scant reward for her unavailing efforts. Your boy has literary taste, but wishes to be an engineer, and success in that profession implies proficiency in mathematics for which he has no adequate capacity. He must be born again in order to achieve the fulfilment of his hopes. A young man tells me that he wishes to learn to be a poet. Literary culture will help him, but no amount of it will enable him to transcend the law that the poet is born and not made. If he is born a poet and does not sing, he will "die with all his music in him"; but if he is not born a poet he will never sing unless he is born again. So in the moral and spiritual life. Marvel not, said the Saviour, that I said unto you, ye must be born again. But with the new life comes the continued influence of the spirit of God witnessing with our spirit that we are born again. So endowed, Peter can then say to us, "Add to your faith virtue, to virtue knowledge, to knowledge temperance, to temperance patience, to patience godliness, to godliness brotherly kindness, and to brotherly kindness charity." Let us not rest with the thought that Christ died for us. Take with it the doctrine of the inward work of the Holy Spirit. To the objective work which Christ accomplished on the Cross, add the doctrine of the new life in regeneration and the growing life of Christian experience. The Spirit helpeth our infirmities and it is by his help that we are enabled to perfect holiness in the fear of the Lord.

These are the two mysteries of salvation: God the Son in the likeness of human flesh standing without us and one of us, and God the Spirit in union with our souls quickening us, leading us into all truth and revealing himself in us. Sin is a crime; sin also is a disease. We need pardon, and we need cure. A man under sentence of death is stricken with pneumonia. Of what avail would a pardon be if he die of the disease? Of what avail a cure if he be executed? The double nature of redemption is pictured here. So with true appreciation of what Christianity means Toplady said,

> Be of sin the double cure;
> Cleanse me from its guilt and power.

(3) *Faith.* In the two things which have been considered we have the whole plan of salvation from the divine point of view. Why then does not God proclaim a general amnesty? The ransom price is paid, the debt has been liquidated, the sac-

rifice has been offered. Why may we not say that all men are saved? It would be enough to answer that this is not the divine plan as Paul expounds it. But if we seek to justify the ways of God to man we may say that it is rational to suppose that the gift, being offered, should be accepted, that the recipient should show gratitude and have confidence in the giver. This is what we are asked to do and all we are asked to do. This is the meaning of justification by faith. Something has been done for us; something is done in us; there is something that we must do. We must believe. Believe in the Lord Jesus Christ and thou shalt be saved. Let us then consider what faith is.

In the opening stanzas of his "In Memoriam" Tennyson seems to state three antitheses: faith and knowledge, faith and sight, faith and proof. But in each case the antithesis is more apparent than real. We believe what we cannot prove, but we also believe what we can prove; we believe what we cannot see, but we believe also what we do see; we believe what we do not know, but we believe also what we do know. But faith covers a wider area than either sight or proof or knowledge. We believe that two and two are four, that the earth is round, that Caesar met his death at the hands of Brutus on the Ides of March; each however for a different reason. We believe some things because they are self-evident, others because they are necessary conclusions reached by deductive logic, others still because they are the results of inductive logic, and yet again others because they rest on sufficient testimony. By all of these methods we reach a state of mind which is expressed by saying, We believe. There are beliefs too which are not adequately supported or have no support at all. The essential feature of faith or belief is that it is a mental state of conviction, whatever the reason for it may be, or whether or no it has any reason. But we are not dealing with unreasonable faith.

Some say that faith is belief on testimony. But this can hardly be correct. I believe that Jones is telling me the truth. But on whose testimony do I believe it? On the testimony of Smith, perhaps. But on whose testimony do I rely when I believe Smith's statement that Jones is a truthful man. You see that if we accept the proposition that faith is a belief on testimony, we shall be off on the trip up the infinite series with which Jonathan Edwards has made us familiar. What are the facts? We believe, this being a generalization based on experience, that a man usually speaks the truth. Sometimes he does not: he may not know; he may be mistaken; he may have a selfish reason for not telling the truth. Take now this general trustworthiness of men and qualify it by those reasons which men have for not telling the truth. Classify these reasons which have revealed themselves in judicial experience, and the result will be a book on

the law of evidence—Starkie, Stephen, Best, or
Greenleaf.   In this book you will find certain pre-
sumptions, some conclusive, some inconclusive.   If
a man admits what is against his interest, you need
go no further for proof.   A man is presumed to in-
tend the natural consequences of his action.   If he
points a gun at another man and kills him, it is presumed that he meant to kill him.   But the death
may have been accidental.   The prisoner has a right
to clear himself and it is the State's duty to see that
he has the benefit of counsel.   In Christianity all
the forms of faith have place: intuition, deduction,
induction, and historical testimony.

Faith is assent to propositions; it is also trust
in a person.   There is a difference between *assensus*
and *fiducia*.   There are no degrees of assent, but
there are many degrees of trust; the reason being
that one is cold intellectual acquiescence in the truth
of a proposition, the other is warm and emotional
trust in a person.   It is common to say that there
are degrees of assent—weak, strong, and confident.
But I think that Cardinal Newman has shown that
what we call degrees of assent to the same proposition are really simple assents to different propositions.   When I say it may rain, it is likely to rain,
it is morally certain to rain to-day, I am not giving
various degrees of assent to the same proposition,
but a simple assent to several different propositions.

When you say the Apostle's Creed you are giving
your assent to a series of propositions.   But when

a man says in his will, 'I trust the keeping of my soul to God,' there is something more than assent. To be a Christian is to assent to certain propositions, but it is more; it is trust. Let us look then at faith under the conception of trust. All of us have this feeling of trust in some form. A man may even trust himself. One cannot stand long on one foot; but he can walk ten miles and be on one foot all the time. Ask him now to walk across the Hudson river on a bridge of planks only eighteen inches wide. He cannot do it. He says, 'I cannot trust myself.' If he lose confidence in his powers of muscular coördination he will fall; for walking is a series of incipient falls as we see in the child when he is learning to walk. Paul was stating a physiological fact as well as a spiritual truth when he said, We walk by faith.

A man trusts himself, but he trusts others sometimes more than he does himself. He has a sum of money that represents the savings of a lifetime. He wishes to invest it where it will be safe. Business is too hazardous. Alluring promises of rich returns from stock transactions do not attract him. He is not drawn to the war bonds of European nations by the high rate of interest. So he buys the securities of the United States Government. The interest, to be sure, is small, but the capital is safe. So Paul trusted the fortune of his soul to God. "I know whom I have believed, and am persuaded that is able to keep that which I have committed to his care." In asking men to trust Christ, the Gospel is only asking them to act toward him who died for us as we act toward our fellow men every day. In individual, national, and international relations men must trust each other. In the everyday life of acquaintance, friendship, blood-relation, up to the hallowed bond of husband and wife, faith manifests itself in ways that can best be described as trust. This is the Gospel. Salvation is a purchased possession, but we pay no part of the price. You cannot divide the cost of it with God.

A father turns over a very valuable piece of property to his daughter, the consideration mentioned in the deed being one dollar. Can that child say that she bought the property? The purchase money was so little that it only emphasized the fact that the property was a gift. Could she say that she had contributed to the purchase? No, for in her own right she was not worth a penny. The very dollar—if she paid it—was given her by her father. So Paul says, "By grace are ye saved through faith; and that not of yourselves; it is the gift of God." In this matter of salvation we are treated as though we had never sinned. There is nothing that we are required to do, or can do. We are justified by faith without the works of the law. We cannot boast or take credit to ourselves. Salvation is a gift; we can only receive it. What could this daughter do? She could be grateful to her father; be more loving and dutiful than ever; trust him more confidently than ever; but she can do nothing regarding the gift. That transaction is closed. So we can say "Thanks be unto God for his unspeakable gift." To do this, however, is to exercise faith. It is to trust. Do we trust? If we do, we need not fear. "Being justified by faith we have peace with God through our Lord Jesus Christ."

But because we are saved by grace it would be a very unworthy thing for one to say 'I have no duties; am no longer under obligation to be sober, honest and industrious; to be pure-minded, generous and full of loving-kindness.' The man who is trusting shows in that act that he has a new nature. Old things have passed away. "How shall we that are dead to sin, live any longer therein?" The man who has been saved by grace will surely feel the obligation to live as God would have him live, and as best he can, to be like God. Being much forgiven he should love much. No argument is needed to make this duty clear. But it will not be easy to do this. We shall have "fightings without and fears within." There will be a conflict between the good nature and the old evil nature. A man will find that "when he would do good evil is present with him"; and the wonderful thing is that the same faith which delivers us from the curse of the law, delivers us also from the power of sin. So we read in the eleventh chapter of the Epistle to the Hebrews what a wonderful rôle faith has had in the history of human life. It goes into every phase of our experience. "Through faith we understand that the worlds were framed by the word of God, so that things which are seen were not made of things which do appear." We must trust our rational nature, and trust our senses, or we shall start with an incurable skecticism. We must trust the laws of nature, or we shall cast doubt upon all the conclusions of inductive science. We must trust human testimony, or we shall make history worthless; trust our own ability to overcome difficulties, trust God to help us in our fight against our own sinful propensities. Read in the chapter just referred to what was accomplished by those "who through faith subdued kingdoms, wrought righteousness, obtained promises, stopped the mouths of lions, quenched the violence of fire, escaped the edge of the sword, out of weakness were made strong, waxed valiant in fight, turned to flight the armies of the aliens."

"This," said the apostle John, "is the victory that overcometh the world, even our faith." Faith justifies, faith also sanctifies. Not everyone who believes can give a reason for the faith that is in him; nor is it necessary for him to do so. The worth of faith does not consist in the way it comes. Your boy gets zero for each of two sums in arithmetic; in the one case because he got a right answer by a wrong method, in the other because he got a wrong answer by a right method.

His exercise was intended to test his knowledge. But it is not so with faith. Your surgeon tells you that you must undergo an operation. Just why, you do not know; just what it is, you do not understand; just how it cures, you cannot tell. But you lie down upon the operating table and take the ether. Teeth out, tonsils out, appendix out, gall bladder out, as the case may be; you put your life in the surgeon's hand and trust. Do you understand the faith which asks no reasons? How blessed it is to think that the ignorant man who cannot learn, the capable man who has not taken time to learn, the dying man who has no chance to learn, can be saved by a faith they do not understand? Surely it was for such that Jesus said, "Blessed are they who have not seen and yet believe." Men differ in their modes of worship. Some prefer a simple service; others are attracted by symbolism. We use these differences about sacraments, vestments, ritual and holy days, to emphasize a feeling of separation from our brethren. But let us get behind these differences and realize the greater importance of the common faith in a crucified and risen Lord out of which these differences arose and to which they bear witness.

Nor need we ask when faith begins or what its history is in any human soul. It may exist in a latent form, exist in spite of its denial. An unquiet conscience is sometimes evidence of an unacknowledged faith. Men sometimes protest too much, and thereby reveal a mental state at variance with their words. Sometimes a man after fruitless effort to solve the problem of destiny will discover that the only thing he can do is to trust. Happy, indeed, is he who thus discovers that the only thing he can do is all he is asked to do! Blessed is the man who after vain endeavour to justify himself, to banish fear, to quiet an accusing conscience, has found in simple trust the master key that opens all the doors of hope. The Church, sacraments, services, Christian fellowships, Christian activity, and the daily struggle against sin, are important helps. But for peace of mind we need not go beyond the precincts of our own consciousness. "The word is nigh thee, even in thy mouth, and in thy heart: that is, the word of faith, which we preach; that if thou shalt confess with thy mouth the Lord Jesus, and shalt believe in thine heart that God hath raised him from the dead, thou shalt be saved."

iii

PAUL'S CRITICS

Are you ready to accept this Pauline doctrine of sin and salvation? If not, it is easy to imagine what you will say.

1. A man may say that he denies the whole of the Pauline conception of Christianity. To say this, however, is to repudiate history; to affirm that Paul's work was based on a complete misap-

prehension of the facts; that Christ did not rise from the dead, was not a divine person, and made no atonement; and that Paul was wrong in his conception of sin and its consequences, and wrong also in his view of the divine purpose and the meaning of Christianity. This, however, involves a complete denial of the facts in Paul's life. But we have no right to make the denial except upon the supposition that Paul wilfully misrepresented them. This supposition, however, is unwarrantable in view of Paul's character, his devotion to his mission, and his self-sacrificing life. If, therefore, men are right in repudiating the Pauline theology, we must believe that the Christian world has lived for nearly two thousand years under a belief that has no warrant; that a fundamental error underlies Christian history; and that the Christian world has been the victim of a monstrous delusion. We must believe that our religion rests on the fundamental facts of Inspiration, Incarnation, Expiation, and Regeneration, or else that the great edifice of Christianity is built upon the sand.

2. A man may say that Paul derived some of his teaching from heathen sources. The soil of the Hellenistic world had been well prepared for the seed of Gospel truth when Paul entered upon his missionary journeys. Philosophy had wrecked the old Olympian theology, and mystery religions imported from Persia and Egypt were taking its place. Men were in that morbid state of mind which often

leads to religious thought. The old joy of life was gone. They were disappointed and dissatisfied. They were looking for a better life or at least for salvation from the troubles of this. Obviously this condition of things was favorable to the spread of the Gospel. In recent years, however, it has been made the basis of a fresh attack upon Christianity, and the attempt has been made to show that Paul derived some of the most conspicuous elements of his teaching from the mystery religions. The word 'salvation' will illustrate the character of this movement. In itself considered, it matters little whether Paul received this word from the mystery religions or whether the latter borrowed it from him. If he found a community in which popular thought sought expression in the word 'salvation' it would be very natural for him to say, 'I hear you speaking of salvation. That is the very subject which has brought me here. I have come to tell you that what you seek is found in Christ and can be found nowhere else.' It does not follow, however, that because two opposite faiths hold certain specific words in common, these words were borrowed by either from the other, or that if they were borrowed they had the same meaning in both communities. A minister of the gospel in our day may use an expression like 'social tissue' or 'survival-value' which has been coined in the agnostic mint; but that does not prove that he is an agnostic, any more than it follows that because

Lincoln at Gettysburg spoke of 'a new birth of freedom,' he was referring to the Christian doctrine of regeneration. If Paul baptized the word 'salvation' into the Christian faith, we may be sure that it was the word which changed its meaning and not the apostle who had changed his faith.

But the supposition that Paul borrowed the vocabulary of the mystery religions as the vehicle of his message is altogether gratuitous; and it is absurd to suppose that the doctrines of Christianity were derived from heathen sources. The two religions which were brought into contact by the apostle's missionary labors were the poles apart. There was but little common ground between Mithraism and Christianity. The former was subjective, the latter objective. The former depended on mystic vision, the latter appealed to historic fact. The former had secrets into which converts were initiated, the latter proceeded by open confession of faith in Christ. The former was mainly a matter of feeling, the latter was based on intellectual apprehension. The former dealt in cult and ceremony, the latter was summed up in faith. More than this I need not say. Those, however, who are interested in this subject should read Dr. Machen's "Sprunt Lectures,"[1] in which they will find a masterly refutation of the theory that Paul's conception of Christianity was in any sense coloured by what he saw of the mystery religions in

[1] J. G. Machen, *The Origin of Paul's Religion*, Chap. VII.

the midst of which he preached the gospel of Christ.

3. Or again, a man may say, 'No, I do not repudiate Paul's teaching—my position is that just as Paul modernized Judaism by refusing to accept circumcision as the law of Christianity in the Gentile world, so we are trying to modernize Christianity by stripping it of the Jewish element of sacrifice which Paul kept and made the basis of his theology.' But the modernist is wrong if he flatters himself that he is in any sense Paul's successor. He argues that Paul fitted the sacrifices of the Jewish ritual to the work of Christ, and that if he discarded one element of Judaism the modernist of to-day has a right to discard another. But here he errs, for he is arguing on the supposition that the sacrificial character of Christ's death is based on analogical reasoning. This is not true. The modernist is trying to explain Christianity by Judaism, but on the contrary it is Judaism that is explained by Christianity. The epistle to the Hebrews was written to show this. "It was not possible that the blood of bulls and of goats should take away sins." The Jewish system was a preparation for Christ, finds its explanation in Christ, and by anticipation derived its value from the sacrifice of Christ. So says the author of the epistle to the Hebrews. The Jewish system was "the bringing in of a better hope"; "that they (the Jews) without us (Christianity) should not be made perfect." To reverse the relations between Judaism and

Christianity, as some are trying to do, is in direct violation of the principles on which Christianity is founded. The modernist pays himself an unmerited compliment in supposing that he is finishing Paul's work by ridding Christianity of some of "the weak and beggarly elements" which escaped Paul's notice.

4. Yet another man may say that he accepts the Christian doctrines even as Paul taught them, with the understanding, however, that these doctrines are to be regarded as value-judgments. In this way he may offer a plausible plea for his position and even publish his system of value-judgments as an *irenicon* to settle the disputes among the theologians. He may say: 'You tolerate different theories of the atonement now. Why not tolerate our view also, which will comprehend them all?' The answer is obvious. These differences of opinion referred to, are based upon different interpretations of Scripture, but with a fundamental agreement among those who differ that the Scriptures are authoritative. Your view does not pretend to be an interpretation of Scripture, but is something imposed upon the Scripture in spite of its direct statements.

But to return to the value-judgment. It is the surviving remnant of a faith once believed on exegetical grounds. It is the giving up of what the Scriptures say, for what they suggest. It is taking the subjective worth of what the Scripture is to you, for what gives it worth. The doctrine may have value, that is one thing; but to make the value a doctrine is a different thing. That the cat may have a grin is conceivable; but the 'grin without the cat' was puzzling to 'Alice.' The Ritschlian is repeating the story of the old fable and dropping the substance of doctrine in his effort to grasp the shadow. The value-judgment is the ghost of a dead faith. It is the unsatisfactory memory of a banquet. It is an inviting odor that mocks the taste. "Who can hold a fire in his hand by thinking on the frosty Caucasus, or cloy the hungry edge of appetite by bare imagination of a feast?"

5. Still another critic of Paul's theology must be heard. It cannot be said of him that he substitutes thought for reality, an idea for the actual. Our objection to his position is not that his theory has no basis in reality but that there is so little of reality in it. He says that Paul misunderstood the sacrifice of Christ, and that in its ultimate meaning it was simply a means of proclaiming the duty of self-sacrifice, and a stimulus to moral endeavour. This is a very common belief; and ever since it was proclaimed by Horace Bushnell and McLeod Campbell it has had many advocates. No new meaning has been put into it by more recent writers, and it cannot be said that Mr. Moberly has aided the cause of the moral influence theory of the atonement by offering Mr. Peggotty's sorrow

as a parallel to the sufferings of Christ. In the interpretation of Calvary it is safe to say that we can get no help from either Edward Caird or Charles Dickens. The moral influence theory of the atonement stands condemned when looked at in the dry light of reason and commonsense.

It is heroic to accept death rather than renounce convictions. But to die simply to make an impression is only a foolish dramatic display. If Jesus died, the just for the unjust, the crucifixion was the greatest incentive to moral courage the world has ever witnessed. But if he died for no other purpose than to illustrate the principle of self-sacrifice, it was a needless act which cut him off in the midst of his days and while, humanly speaking, his work was still unfinished. If a man must accept death in battle as the price of his country's liberty, he is a hero; but if he dies without any reason and simply to show men how they ought to die when there is a reason, he is only exhibiting an irrational foolhardiness. If a man drowns in the act of saving a drowning child he is a hero. But if he drowns himself simply to show how much he loves a friend, his act so far from exerting an exemplary influence will only excite ridicule. It is strange that men can find anything meritorious in "the death of the Cross" after they have eliminated the only reason that can justify it.

6. Again, it will be said that Christianity is a 'regulative faith.' There is a certain amount of

force in this statement. It would be impossible for us to understand truths which transcend earthly experience if they were not presented to us in the language of our daily life. Let us concede the truth embodied in the idea of a 'regulative faith,' and let us be thankful that God has presented to us the truths pertaining to eternal life in terms that we can understand. Heaven is described as a city. Its walls rise up in our imagination; its gates are numbered; its employments are described; and the happiness of its holy inhabitants is set forth in lofty and majestic terms. This you say is regulative faith. If it is, then this is the way in which God means that we shall think of heaven. Would you change this regulative faith for one of your own making? What would you do? Would you modernize the metaphors of Scripture? Would you install a modern orchestra in heaven and dress the redeemed in the prevailing fashion? Have we not gone as far already in this direction as good taste will allow us? Would you address the Father in Heaven as many people allow children to address their parents, with the free familiarity which as often breeds contempt as it fosters love? Are we not shocked sometimes when the language of devotion takes on the banal form of earthly endearment, or lapses into the informality of casual conversation? Are we not in danger of losing a sense of the divine majesty in our unstudied and random emotionalism, in the idle information we give the Almighty, in our tedious recitals, in the disjointed prattle we utter in his presence, in the turgid rhetoric we pour into his ear? Is this the way that you would construct a regulative faith to supersede the lofty speech of Scripture?

Or will you seek by a process of distillation to put the basal truths of Scripture in smaller compass? Will you try to embody the essentials of Christianity in large generalizations where all figurative language is translated into philosophic diction and its amplified utterances on sin and redemption are expressed in terms of logical exactness? Then you will remove Christianity from the easy apprehension of the common mind, and instead of the warmth of feeling and the glow of enthusiasm which characterize the utterances of Scripture, we shall have a few cold and pompous propositional statements which exhale no aroma of piety and awaken no feeling of devotion.

In either case you will fail. In your attempt to bring heaven down to earth you will vulgarize the solemn language of Scripture; and your supposed distillation will turn out to be a commonplace dilution resulting in a confusion of thought, and the consequent delusion that the greater the dilution the greater its potency will be. Let us not be deceived by what Robert South called "the fatal imposture and force of words." There are two kinds of regulative faith, one which consists in believing that "the half has not been told us," the other in rejecting half of what the Scriptures have to say. The difference between the two is the difference between accepting and rejecting Christianity.

iv

PAUL'S ORBIT

The man who keeps a small shop and whose thoughts are limited to the purchase of goods and their sale at a profit has a very limited range of mental vision. But his competitor in the same form of business activity begins to expand his transactions and as he does so comes to see that the whole globe is engaged in this enterprise of bargain and sale, that he is a partner in a great system of mercantile exchange, and that questions of soil, climate, weather, supply and demand, conditions of peace or war, and facilities of transportation are active elements in determining his success. In this way, and from a particular point of view, he comes to realize the interconnectedness of physical phenomena within his own sphere of observation.

A man who is engaged in the minute study of the lower forms of life may be so absorbed in his favorite pursuit as to miss the great truth which his studies should teach him, and may be blind to the meaning of Tennyson's parable of the "flower in the crannied wall." But if he follow the leading of his reason he will see that to know the organism which is the object of his research he must know other things as well, and that a complete survey of his own field will require him to trespass on his neighbor's property. In this way he will come to understand the inter-relations of all forms of life, and see that physically speaking nature is a totality the parts of which are not only mechanically connected as antecedents and consequents; but that antecedents are in order to consequents, as means to ends, and that a purposive trend is visible throughout the material world. It will make a difference in his religious beliefs whether he interprets this purposive trend in the terms of theism, or pantheism, or panpsychism; but the whole scheme of science when it is properly understood, is in keeping with the idea that divine purpose is the key which unlocks the mystery of nature.

To see purpose, however, is to see selection for the accomplishment of ends, and this is Paul's generic conception which runs through all his writings. If we confine ourselves to nature we shall see that she has her favorites and that "of fifty seeds she often brings but one to bear"; that according to a prevailing doctrine of evolution, natural selection explains the rising scale of physical shapes and psychical endowments; and that the system of selection goes through the history of races and determines the lot of individual members of a community. Differences of original endowment, conditions of life, lack of education, lack of opportunity, explain many of the differences existing among men. Some start in the handicap race of life with obvious reasons for their distinction; others with the same natural potentialities are too heavily weighted to win. Shelley and Keats were gifted men, but they did not live out half their days, and what they left is only an earnest of what they might have done. By insight and foresight some men take advantage of opportunity and rise to wealth and power, while others who do not know how to 'take occasion by the hand' are left to spend their lives in the ordinary mediocrities of business.

This selection of favorites does not stop here, but finds expression in political life; but now we drop the first letter of our descriptive word and the process goes on under another name. Men set up a government on the principle that all men are born free and equal, with results which show that however free they are, they are not equal, save in their political franchises. Every American-born boy has a right to hope that he may be President of the United States. The hope may be a useful spur to his ambition; but as we can have only twenty-five Presidents in a century—with an allowance of slight variation, due to the accident which may give the country two Presidents in one term, or to popular favour which may give one President two terms —the chances against any one boy out of a hundred million being elected to the Presidency are enormously great. But it is election which puts the chief magistrate of the Republic in his place. In all matters connected with honor, office and emolument, election is a very familiar word; but taken in connection with selection it serves to show how the correlative idea of purpose must needs be a great constructive conception in our interpretation of the universe.

"Purpose" is a dominant word in Paul's theology. His theory of the universe was that of God's purpose translated into reality. Paul, however, was not constructing a theory of the universe. His orbit was not a circle, with God as the centre, and the boundary of being as its circumference. It was rather an ellipse, determined by the two foci of an eternal purpose and an eternal prospect.

1. ETERNAL PURPOSE. Paul's interpretation of Christianity was under the conception of eternal purpose. This purpose embraced the entire history of the human race, from its creation to the achievement of its destiny. It is not strange, then, that following the example of Paul, theologians have made the divine purpose their starting-point in systematic theology. I am not saying that this is the best, or that it is the only mode of organizing the material given us in revelation. But it is a logical and perhaps the most logical method. I do not enter into any comparisons of that kind. In the work of organizing the teachings of Scripture into systems of theology the Reformed theologians hold

a very conspicuous place, though a great deal of work has been done by Lutheran theologians, and perhaps it may be said that in recent years they have taken the lead in the production of systems of dogmatic theology. We must not forget, moreover, that long before the Reformation the Schoolmen, notably Aquinas, had dealt with this subject very minutely. Roman Catholic theologians through such representative men as Bellarmine of an older day and Perrone of a later time, have also done important work in systematic theology. But nowhere among English speaking people has such conspicuous attention been given to the construction of systems of theology as we find in the works of the American theologians—Hodge, H. B. Smith, Thornwell, Shedd, Dabney and Breckenridge; all of them belonging to the Calvinistic school. The absorbing interest in historico-critical studies has to a great extent diverted the attention of scholars from systematic theology. The effect of this is seen in the pulpit to-day. If our young ministers would seriously undertake to rethink for themselves the meaning of Christianity on the broad lines of the Pauline theology, I feel sure that it would mean the dawning of a new day in the preaching of the Gospel.

If now this purposive idea is made the starting point of a systematized statement of the contents of Scripture it is easy to see that creation, sin, redemption, and eternal life must be treated under this eternal purpose. The result of this is that individual salvation unto eternal life is part of that eternal purpose, however conditioned it may be by man's free agency, and however free agency may be limited by a corrupt nature. This, however, is no new doctrine. That salvation is the free gift of God, and that ability to do what we are required to do is due to the grace of God, follow by logical consequence from Augustine's doctrine of original sin and are implied in his famous petition: *Da quod jubes et jube quod vis.*

Beginning then with the doctrine of God's eternal purpose, men have inquired whether this purpose contemplated men before or after the Fall; that is to say, whether provision for human salvation was made in view of the possibility of the race's lapse, or whether that provision contemplated the lapse with all its consequences. Hence we have had in the Calvinistic school of theologians supralapsarianism and sublapsarianism, each being a combination of speculative thought and exegetical support. I cannot pretend to have much interest in these speculations and I do not think that an exposition of them would interest those who are likely to read what I have to say.

The Augustinian or Calvinistic system of theology starting with the divine purpose as its premise, was opposed by those who took exception to the idea that the faith which justifies is included in the divine intention and is therefore a divine gift.

Then came the Synod of Dort and the extrusion of the Remonstrant party from the Reformed body. I am not discussing the question whether the Reformed body should ever have found in the Remonstrant theology a reason for disruption into Arminian and Calvinistic forms of faith. But I prefer to regard these two sections of the Reformed faith as generically one; with a specific difference in regard to the election of individuals into eternal life, both parties agreeing that the eternal purpose of God is the fundamental conception in the systematic exhibition of the Scriptural doctrine of salvation, while they differ on the question whether we should say with the Calvinists that justifying faith is implied in the doctrine of election, or with the Arminians that election to eternal life is on the ground of a foreseen faith. It would be difficult I think to divide a church at the present day on this issue. The Calvinistic position has always been that a contingency cannot be foreseen. On the other hand, Arminians have always argued that foreknowledge does not imply foreordination. Into this field of debate I do not propose to enter. But when the Arminian position is defended, as at the present day it sometimes is, on the ground that God determined not to know who would believe, men only add another difficulty to a question which is already sufficiently burdened, and are really defending their position on a basis which would have made it possible for the incarnation to have taken place and the atonement to have been made without there being any favorable response to the Gospel's invitation. But the possible failure of Christianity from the beginning is an hypothesis which it is hard, and for some men, impossible to entertain. The raising of this question brings us into a sphere of thought which is incomprehensible and presents a problem in regard to liberty and ability to which the Scriptures offer no solution. On this subject, however, I venture to offer a few words.

When you wish to go from the Battery to Central Park you have a choice of three roads: the subway, the surface, and the elevated. A stranger, let us suppose, gets on the subway express and starts for Fifty-ninth street. He finds his place and the train starts. This passenger is shut up in an iron box, the tunnel is dark, and he is alone. He finds himself in the grip of a system of pre-arranged machinery. He cannot get out. He does not know in what direction he is going, and finally the train stops. He has reached his journey's end and he must get out. This is human life from a naturalistic point of view, according to which from the beginning of life's journey to its close one is in the iron grip of a set of physical antecedents and consequents. Paul never took this road.

Then there is the elevated road. A man gets on the train, sits at a window, and looks down upon the stream of human life below. Men cross the street, some at right angles, some obliquely. They run in front of passing motor cars and risk their lives to save a moment's time. Some stop, and their motions seem to indicate that they are engaged in conversation. But this is all inference, for the passenger hears no voices. He is looking at a moving picture. These human beings, trucks, horses and motor cars present a strange medley of motions as they dodge each other like a swarm of flies, and like flies, too, without collision. They have the appearance of marionettes moved by invisible strings and guided by a hidden hand. Ordinarily Paul did not take this mode of travel, or as we say "the high priori road," but sometimes he did. You will find passages in the 'Romans' and 'Ephesians' where you feel sure that he was travelling on 'the elevated.' Everything in sight, everything past and future is arranged according to a purpose, happens in fulfilment of a purpose, and points to a purpose to be realized.

But for ordinary travel Paul took the 'surface car' where he was in constant contact with human beings. He talked with them, listened to their words, heard about their plans, and knew of their troubles. He noticed how confidently they spoke of what they had done, were going to do, and what other men were doing or trying to do in opposition to them. He would sometimes talk with men who had been disappointed or badly treated; who wondered why their lot had been so hard, or felt that some power unseen and over them had directed all things for the best. These men revealed that they had conflicting ideas in their minds; and that the stream of their lives held two opposing elements in solution and that now one, now the other, was precipitated. Paul realized this conflict in the lives of men; knew that there were some things which men ought to do but could not do, and he comforted them with the promise of divine aid. He knew that of themselves they would not do what he desired them to do, yet he entreats them to do it. Paul saw the antimony between freedom and divine purpose. This seeming contradiction between human depravity and moral obligation Paul realized, but he made no attempt to explain it. If everything is included in the divine purpose there can be no contingency. Of this there can be no doubt. But must a man be a philosophical determinist in regard to the will in order to be a Calvinist? Jonathan Edwards seemed to think so, and his theory of the will is really a philosophical defence of Calvinistic theology. It is hard to escape the force of the Edwardian logic, though it may be said with some force that in transferring the idea of cause and effect from physical events to the successive states of the mind, instead of finding the idea of cause in will and its spontaneities, the doctrine of determinism has been made to rest upon a wrong view of causation. Paul does not solve this antinomy between divine purpose and human freedom. And whether men are determinists or indeterminists it is hard for them to be consistent, as may be shown by abundant illustration.

Put, for example, an Arminian and a Calvinist in the same pulpit, the one to pray and the other to preach. The Arminian will in all probability beseech God, who turneth the hearts of men as he turneth the rivers of water, to give men grace to believe, and enable them to accept the offer of salvation; and the Calvinist when he has reached the point of fervent exhortation will urge men to believe in Christ regardless of his doctrine of inability and his philosophical determinism. In other words, the Arminian is to all intents and purposes a Calvinist when he prays, and the Calvinist an Arminian when he preaches. But this apparent contradiction is a common feature of religious thought. I do not suppose that Father Knox is a Calvinist, but he plainly recognizes faith as a gift and attributes his belief in the resurrection of Christ to the grace of God. I do not suppose that Faber was a Calvinist, yet Calvinistic theology is embodied in his beautiful hymn:

> O gift of gifts! O grace of faith,
>   My God, how can it be
> That Thou, Who hast discerning love,
>   Shouldst give that gift to me?
>
> How many hearts Thou mightst have had
>   More innocent than mine,
> How many souls more worthy far
>   Of that sweet touch of Thine!

2. ETERNAL PROSPECT. But Paul lived also under the influence of an eternal hope that was to find its realization in a future life. Drop this idea of immortality, and what avails it to believe in an eternal purpose? Men toil, have disappointments, meet reverses, endure pain, foster high ideals of conduct, and die. Suppose that this is the end of all things to every man. Can you feel that it is worth while to have lived under these conditions? Does not this effort, this perseverance in the presence of failure, suggest to us a better life? Is not this discipline intended to serve a moral purpose that is to be realized in us? Convince men that death means extinction of being, would they then have courage to endure the great "fight of affliction?" What purpose can it serve to bear this weight of suffering? What mean these strivings after something higher, better, and more enduring if there awaits us no career? Paul felt this and saw the logical consequences of scepticism in regard to immortality, saw that a man might surrender himself to a life of pleasure if the future offered no hope. "If after the manner of men, I have fought with beasts at Ephesus, what advantageth it me, if the dead rise not? Let us eat and drink for tomorrow we die." He put the whole of the hedonist's case in these words. His doctrine of immortality was the logical concomitant of the divine purpose. Accordingly he presents these two ideas in close connection with each other. When writ-

ing to Timothy he says: "Be thou partaker of the afflictions of the gospel according to the power of God; who hath saved us, and called us with an holy calling, not according to our works, but according to his own purpose and grace, which was given us in Christ Jesus, before the world began; but is now made manifest by the appearing of our Saviour Jesus Christ, who hath abolished death, and hath brought life and immortality to light through the gospel."

But what is the character of this eternal life? We commonly speak of it under the two forms of thought, Time and Space. The mind ordinarily regards death as a transfer to another point in space. We think of it as embarking for another shore and wonder what our environment will be. We have the common idea that location determines our pleasure. We do not, as a rule, think that a man's life consisteth not in the abundance of the things which he possesseth, and that it is what he is and not where he is, that is important.

But there are times with most of us when satisfaction is found in simple consciousness, regardless of weather, wealth, luxury, or any material conditions. Paul seems to have had this idea. To be sure he spoke of his 'inheritance,' and of being 'with Christ,' and those words imply spatial relations; but in the main it was the unending character of the future life which occupied his thought. His mind moved in the category of time rather than

of space. Time, however, can be considered under
the two conceptions of measured and unmeasured
duration. Locke defined time as "certain portions
of eternity set out in measures." This conception
of time would not be regarded as satisfactory now,
but the distinction between measured and unmeasured duration is easily understood. We have a
good illustration of this difference in "In Memoriam":

> Old Yew, which graspeth at the stones
>   That name the under-lying dead,
>   Thy fibres net the dreamless head,
> Thy roots are wrapped about the bones.
>
> The seasons bring the flower again,
>   And bring the firstling to the flock;
>   And in the dusk of thee, the clock
> Beats out the little lives of men.

Men as a rule emphasize measured duration.
They live by the clock. They feel that they must
be employed. They attend a meeting of this
Board and that Board; and rise, watch in hand,
to attend the meeting of another Board. Their
question is how to employ time or to 'kill it.' They
must be busy: at business during business hours,
at golf or bridge afterwards. When they think of
Heaven,—if they ever do,—they wonder what they
will do there, and complain in advance, of the programme, because there is too much singing. Their
idea of time is measured duration. They would
have difficulty in thinking of an eternity that is
not 'set out in measures.' Let us try to think of

this unmeasured duration——of a life where there is no calendar, no dated daily paper, no tick of watch, no beat of pendulum, no 'kiss of toothed wheels,' no flowers of spring, no autumn leaves, no new moon's crescent in the western sky, no sunsets, no yesterdays, no sad memories, no dark forebodings, no failing strength, no fading life, no death. Most men would not be contented with this even and unmeasured flow of unending duration. It is the clock and not the 'sullen tree' which best satisfies their idea of time.

But men are not all alike. There are some who find their highest pleasure in reflection. Whether on the train or on ship-board or in the quiet of their own home, they sometimes have their happiest experiences in hours that pass unnoticed, when thought is out of harness and the mind is free to play with its own spontaneities. These men are often classed as idle people by those whose movements are determined for them in advance and who are the slaves of the clock.

As life goes in this world a compromise between these two modes of living would be best for all of us. The brooding man would be better for more exercise and companionship; the busy man, if he gave more time to reflection. It is not understood as well as it should be that idleness is often the seed-plot of thought. If a man is to succeed in his best endeavours, let him guard his moments of un-companioned silence. Let him take time to open

the windows of his soul and be on the watch for
thoughts that drift in he knows not whence or
how. This is particularly true of those who do the
work which the minister is called to do.

To those who know what good work means,
what variety of information, power of constructive thought, and carefulness of speech the minister's duties imply, the wonder is that the men in
this holy calling accomplish half of what they do.
Think of what the life of a minister is. He is
the rich man's almoner, the poor man's friend; he
has an open ear for the soliciting representative of a
'cause' who wants a key that will open the door of
interview with a benevolent banker; he makes visits
innumerable, solemnizes marriages, and conducts
funerals; edits the church calendar, keeps an eye on
his congregation's benevolences, has Board meetings
to attend, committee meetings to preside over;
speeches to make, schemes of municipal reform to
coöperate with, colleges and universities to visit;
and at the end of a week of weariness must hold
his nerves in leash preparatory to the two sermons
he is to deliver on Sunday. His people come to
hear him, expecting to be guided by his counsel,
warmed by his fervor, moved by his eloquence,
and stimulated by his example. They look for a
sermon that implies culture, scholarship, and a delicate sense of literary form. They watch the constructive clearness of his argument and wait for the
"jewels five words long" which at one moment

or another are sure to sparkle in the pulpit; and if they happen to be disappointed they tell the visiting friend who went to church with them that their minister was 'not up to the mark this morning.' How often, my ministerial friend, has your best morning been spoiled by interruptions? You had a thought which you wished to elaborate. It had been in your mind two or three times already, but before you could define its shape it had passed out of sight. You have dwelt upon it in sleepless intervals at night; to-day you were going to give it form. It was to serve a special purpose, and you were keeping it for that. But in the midst of your interruptions it had taken flight, and you can only say in the words of the prophet, "As thy servant was busy here and there it was gone."

You can add and subtract by the clock; make debits and credits by the clock, so much an hour; yes, more than that, or you will lose your job; more yet, or the young man next to you will take your place; and some day in the sombre evening of your life you will go home with the death sentence weighing on your heart in your employer's words, 'We shall not need your services any longer.' Oh, I feel so sorry for those men who live by the clock and under the lash of 'efficiency.'

But you cannot write a poem by the clock with the feeling that you have only five minutes left in which to finish it. You cannot prepare what you would like to say to your congregation on the principle of filling so many sheets of sermon paper in an hour. The demands on the pulpit were never so great as now. The opportunities open to it never greater. To him who has the gifts and feels the spirit of his calling there is no career that can be compared to it, none for which he would leave it; but what he needs is time: time to read, time to organize his thought, time to visit the gallery of his imagination and appraise the pictures that are painted there; time to flee to the uplands and pitch his tent with the poets and philosophers; time to see that a text as he read it yesterday is freighted with a meaning he had never seen before; time to cultivate his feelings and have "a heart at leisure from itself to soothe and sympathize"; time for the transfiguring influence of the Spirit, so that when he comes down from the mount his face will shine by reason of his fellowship with God. Get thee up to the high mountain and stay there, giving no sign of where you are save as now and then, like Arnold's 'high pasturing kine,' the tinkle of a bell shall reveal the place of your retreat. I can well understand therefore that a timeless eternity would not be so dull as men might at first suppose.

The distinction between measured and unmeasured duration may help us in our thought of God. There is measurable duration which lies beyond the limits of our perception, and there is an unmeasured duration, represented by our hours of reverie, when we take no note of time. A wheel

So long Thy power hath blest me, sure it still
    Will lead me on
O'er moor and fen, o'er crag and torrent, till
    The night is gone;
And with the morn those angel faces smile
Which I have loved long since, and lost awhile.

What heaven is like we do not know, for the Scriptures commonly speak of it in negating terms. There is no impurity there, nor anything that loveth or maketh a lie. There will be no sin in heaven, no sorrow, and no more death. And we can easily believe that much that gives us pleasure here will have no place in that abode of bliss. The roads to wealth and power and place will all be closed. There will be no room for pride or envy. The statesman and the soldier will find their occupations gone. There will be no dread of war, and no frantic wish for peace.

And only the Master shall praise us, and only the Master shall
    blame;
And no one shall work for money and no one shall work for fame.

But the great world of values will remain. Truth will not die; and men will still love beauty and goodness. Those who reduce the fair form of religion to a skeleton of intellectual apprehension will find that feeling is an element in religion as well as thought, and that they have missed much by their neglect of that which feeds it. Those who have invested their religious assets in the symbolisms of sound and color will find a joy they

[324]

never knew before in simple apprehension of the truth. Religion then will be a holy synthesis of all that is true and beautiful and good. The "faith" of Paul and the "works" of James, will be transfigured and absorbed in the "love" of John; and all that is great in intellect, will and feeling will find in worship its full fruition. Let us be thankful therefore that the unendingness of the life to come of which Paul spoke is supplemented by the spatial conception of heaven which the beloved disciple gives us in his apocalyptic vision. And though we know that eye hath not seen, nor ear heard, neither have entered into the heart of man the things which God hath prepared for them that love him, let us give play to our imagination under the restricting limitations of the inspired word in thinking of the joy of heaven.

Is it too much to suppose that the experiences of heaven will reveal the limits of religious thought under which our earthly conceptions of truth were formed; that "seeing through a glass darkly" men failed to see that there was error and incompleteness in their so-called systems of truth; that there was an underlying truth in some of the systems which were once called false; and that in the light of eternity men will find a higher unity which will discard the false and conserve the true?

Is it too much to think that seeing "face to face" as then they will, men who find it hard to fit into each other the ragged edges of fragmentary truth,

kingdom to the Father and God shall be all in all:

> That God, which ever lives and loves,
> One God, one law, one element,
> And one far-off divine event
> To which the whole creation moves.

We could listen longer, but the sermon is ended and the service closes with the doxology of the redeemed. "Unto him that loved us and washed us from our sins in his own blood, and hath made us kings and priests unto God and his Father, to him be glory and dominion forever and ever. Amen."

CONCLUSION

In the light of all that can be said in support of Christianity are we not ready to say with Paul, "I am not ashamed of the gospel of Christ: for it is the power of God unto salvation?" Tested by history, science, philosophy, and human experience, does it not vindicate its claims? Are you not glad that proper regard for the facts of Scripture will not allow the worm of Hegelian philosophy to eat the substance out of the leaves of the tree of life and (*pace* Mr. Bradley) leave us only a dessicated web of juiceless categories?

Would you be willing to exchange this substance of historic fact for the shadow of it reflected in Ritschlianism? Would you give up this verte-brated system of religious belief for the structure-less simplicity of any of its rivals? Would you exchange its clear lines of logical coherency for a colloidal compound of good feeling? I hope not. Is there any particular in which you can improve Christianity? Is there any substitute for it which will meet the needs of men and satisfy the facts of history? I think not.

> "What think ye of Christ," friend?
>   When all's done and said
> You like this Christianity or not?
> It may be false, but will you wish it true?
> Has it your vote to be so if it can?

Browning asks a searching question here. It looks as if Christianity were repugnant to so many. It seeks their good and offers them a priceless gift; but they treat it with indifference and are often malignant in their hostility to it. Why then do men not believe? Is it too much to say that they do not wish to believe? I listened once at a philosophical meeting to the reading of a paper on the psychology of the hermit crab. To carry on his investigation the author of the paper put the crab in a box, so arranged that the light might be admitted at the author's pleasure from different directions. The experiment showed that no matter where the crab might be in the box or from what point the light came, the crab invariably moved toward the light. That the crab had very slight intelligence did not surprise me, but that he made such good use of the little sense he had, taught me a very important lesson. A man does not need much knowledge in order to believe. Meagre indeed must a man's intelligence be if it is not enough to enable him to do all that he is asked to do. "Walk in the light and ye shall be the children of light."

Many of us have seen in Keble College, Oxford, Holman Hunt's picture "Christ the light of the world." The night is dark, and the Saviour stands at a cottage door holding in one hand a lantern the light of which is reflected in his lovely face; the other hand is on the door in the act of knocking. You may be solitary and alone on your island of selfhood and you will hear no plash of friendly oar if you wish it so. You may barricade yourself in the mountain fastness of your own personality and need dread no invasion. You may sit alone in the unlighted chambers of your soul and the Saviour will take no unbidden step across your threshold. But this is what he says: "Behold I stand at the door and knock; if any man hear my voice and open the door, I will come in to him, and will sup with him, and he with me."

Feb 1st 1927

INDEX

Anaxagoras, 6.
Anselm, 85-90.
Antitheism, 11-57.
Aquinas, 308.
Archimedes, 6.
Aristotle, 6.
Arnold, Matthew, 51, 62, 185, 229, 248, 257.
Atonement, The, 281-3.
Augustine, St., 85, 213, 308.

Bacon, Lon, 141, 323.
Baden-Powell, 69.
Baillie, J. B., 36 note.
Bain, Alexander, 76.
Balfour, Earl of, 98-9.
Barrier Act, 142.
Behaviourism, 19-22.
Bellarmine, 308.
Bentham, Jeremy, 76.
Berkeley, 27, 51.
Bergson, Professor Henri, 71, 115.
Best, 288.
Bible, The: Truth of, 144-8; authority of, 148-161; inspiration of, 161-173.
Blunt, J. H., 129.
Boethius, 85.
Bosanquet, Boman, 48.
Bradley, F. H., 44-5, 48.

Breckinridge, 308.
Browning, 60, 94, 226, 329.
Brucker, 9.
Bushnell, Horace, 25, 300.
Butler, Bishop, 97.

Cabanis, 16.
Caird, Edward, 39-40, 257.
Calvin, 119, 129.
Campbell, McLeod, 300.
Carr, J. Wildon, 57-8.
Chalcedonian Christology, 209-15; attacked, 216-228.
Christ: as founder, 184-5; teacher, 185-7; example, 187-9; divinity of, 228-244.
Christendom, reunion of, 125-128.
Christian consciousness, 152-6.
Christianity, what? 179-184; Hegelian interpretation of, 191-196; Naturalistic interpretation of, 196-8; Ritschlian interpretation of, 198-208.
Church, The: meaning of, 118-122; function of, 122-138.
Clarke, Samuel, 88.
Clifford, W. K., 101 note.
Croce, Signor Benedetto, 42.

[331]

INDEX

Cunningham, John, 142 note.
Curcellaeus, 159.

Dabney, Dr., 308.
Darwin, 6.
Democritus, 13.
Dewey, John, 42.
Descartes, 46, 88, 143.
Dickens, Charles, 301.
Drews, 220.
Du-Bois, Raymond, 18.
Duff, Robert A., 26 note.

Edwards, Jonathan, 46, 287, 313.
Einstein, 42.
Epicurus, 76.
Eucken, Rudolf, 4 note.

Faber, F. W., 314.
Faith, and Reason, 100; deposit of, 128-131; meaning of, 285-9; salvation by, 289-294.
Fechner, 53.
Ferrier, David, 16.
Ferrier, J. F., 88.
Fiske, John, 23.
Fraser, A. C., 104 note.
Fraser, Sir J. G., 220.

God: see Theism.
Gore, Bishop, 113, 121, 124-5, 152, 214.
Green, T. H., 30, 38-40.
Greenleaf, 288.

Haldane, Viscount, 41-2, 192.
Haldane, J. B. S., 246.
Happel, 9.
Harnack, A. von, 190.
Harper, G. M., 56.
Harris, W. T., 211.
Hartley, David, 16, 179.
Headlam, Bishop, 121, 128 note.
Heaven, 322-328.
Hegel, 28-38, 88, 178.
Herbart, 29.
Hodge, Charles, 136, 231, 308.
Höffding, Dr. Harald, 204.
Howison, Professor, 54.
Hume, 21, 24.
Huxley, T. H., 23, 207.

Ideals, realm of, 84-90.
Incarnation, cosmic effect of, 244-9; and immortality, 249-252.
Inge, Dean, 24-48.

James, William, 1, 37, 53, 55, 79 note.

Kant, 27-8, 30, 62, 71-2, 75, 87-8, 90-92, 199.
Kepler, 52.
Kirkman, T. P., 96.
Knox, Father, 314.

Lake, Dr. Kirsopp, 222, 238.
La Mettrie, 16.
Lange, F. A., 46, 70.

INDEX

Lecky, W. E. H., 132.
Leibnitz, 29.
Leverrier, 100.
Lewes, G. H., 19.
Lewis, Sir G. Cornewall, 135 note.
Liddon, Candu, 232.
Lightfoot, Bishop, 121.
Locke, 56, 317.
Lotze, 29, 61.
Lucretius, 249.

Machan, J. G., 297.
McTaggart, J. E. M., 55-6, 61, 67, 101-2.
Mallock, W. H., 76.
Mansel, Dean, 97-8.
Martineau, James, 26 note.
Masson, Professor, 59.
Materialism, 13-24.
Maudesley, Dr. Henry, 16.
Mill, J. S., 19, 59, 61, 66, 76.
Moberly, R. C., 238.
Moberly, W. H., 45-6, 300.
Moehler, 136.
Morley, Lord, 178.
Muirhead, J. H., 38, 40, 58.
Muller, Max, 9.

New Christianity, the; cause and symptoms of, 174-9.
Newman, Cardinal, 156-7, 288, 324.
Newton, 52.

Pantheism, 24-49.

Parmenides, 24.
Paul, St.: The man, 255-272; letters of, 267-270; speeches of, 270-2; the theologian, 273-294; his critics, 294-304; his orbit, 304-328.
Perrone, 308.
Plato, 6.
Plumptre, C. E., 46.
Pluralism, 49-57.
Pollock, Sir Frederick, 26 note.
Pope, Alexander, 27, 281-2.
Pragmatism, 78-81.
Prall, David W., 106 note.
Pringle-Pattison, 48, 59-60, 64, 198.
Price, Richard, 75.
Prospect, eternal, 314-328.
Punishment, philosophy of, 277-280.
Purpose, eternal, 307-14.

Rashdall, Hastings, 61.
Rawlinson, A. E. J., 121, 128 note.
Raymond de Sebonde, 182.
Reason, the 97; and Faith, 100; and Knowledge, 102; and Religion, 108; and Christianity, 110-116.
Regeneration, 283-5.
Riemann, 42.
Royce, Josiah, 55.
Russell, Bertrand, 79 note.

Sabatier, Auguste, 96.

INDEX

Salvation, 277-294.
Sanday, William, 215.
Shaftesbury, Lord, 75.
Schelling, 9-34.
Schiller, F. C. S,, 37, 79 note.
Schleiermacher, 153.
Shaw, Bernard, 80.
Shedd, W. G. T., 308.
Short, Bishop, 129.
Sidgwick, Henry, 76.
Sin, 273-285.
Smith, Henry B., 308.
Smith, Kemp, 22.
Sorley, Professor, 81.
South, Robert, 303.
Spencer, Herbert, 9, 15, 22-3, 45, 76, 178-9.
Spinoza, 24-27, 61.
Spirit, witness of, 158-161.
Starkie, 288.
Stephen, 288.
Stephen, Sir Leslie, 77.
Strauss, David, 216, 220.

Tennyson, 11, 94, 176, 237, 246, 286, 317, 328.

Theism; origin of, 5-11; incoming of, 57-65; arguments for, 65-90.
Things, realm of, contingency, order, purpose, 66-72.
Thorburn, T. J., 218.
Thornwell, 308.
Time; measured and unmeasured duration, 317-322.
Tutankhamen, 177.

Values; realm of, 72-84; value judgment, 201-205.
Venn, *Logic of Chance*, 68-9.

Ward, Professor James, 17, 56.
Warfield, B. B., 224 note.
Weiss, Johannes, 225.
Wells, H. G., 61.
Westcott, Bishop, 254.
Westermarch, Edward, 77.
Whewell, 185.
Whitman, Walt, 274.
Wordsworth, Bishop, 146.
Wordsworth, William, 56.

Xenophanes, 26.

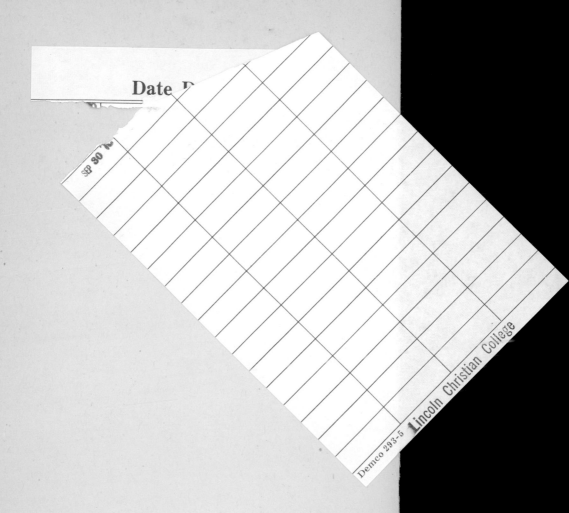